War!
Patrick Henry's Finest Hour,
Lord Dunmore's Worst

Published by Telford Publications*

Design by Andrew Evans Design
Cover illustration by David Eccles

© George T. Morrow II 2012

Telford Publications
301 Mill Stream Way,
Williamsburg, VA, U.S.A., 23185

Tel (757) 565-7215
Fax (757) 565-7216
www.williamsburgincharacter.com

FIRST EDITION

* Telford Publications is named for Alexander Telford,
a volunteer rifleman from Rockbridge County, Virginia, who
served in three Revolutionary War campaigns, in the last of which,
Yorktown, he was personally recognized by Gen. George Washington
for his extraordinary marksmanship with the long rifle.

Library of Congress Control Number: 2012948306
ISBN 978-0-9831468-7-2
Printed and bound by Sheridan Press, 450 Fame Avenue, Hanover, PA

War!

Patrick Henry's Finest Hour,
Lord Dunmore's Worst

George T. Morrow II

WILLIAMSBURG IN CHARACTER

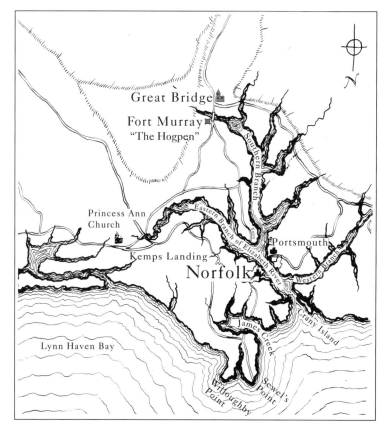

The Theater of War in July, 1775

To Joan

"If a man could say nothing against a character but what he can prove, history could not be written."
SAMUEL JOHNSON

Contents

List of Illustrations

The End of Dunmore

The story you are about read is both comic and tragic, and it is hard to say which predominates. The villain in the piece, Lord Dunmore, does try to get up a proper war, issuing bombastic proclamations, tramping about the countryside at the head of a regiment of British grenadiers and bombarding the homes of former members of his Governor's Council. There are the usual atrocities: the young woman disemboweled by one of Col. Banastre Tarleton's dragoons and left nailed to the door of a house at Jamestown; the death agonies of the scores of slaves who answered Dunmore's call for an army of Ethiopes; and, on the promised lighter note, the spectacle of Capt. Squire of the *Otter*, obstinately clinging to a tree in a hurricane after refusing an invitation from the tree's owner, a rebel, to take shelter in his house.

But it is largely a made-up war, waged by Dunmore for fear of being thought inactive by his masters in the British ministry and inspired by a desire for personal revenge. The promised encounter between Patrick Henry (now Commander in Chief of Virginia's army) fails to come off, Henry having been pointedly left cooling his heels in his war camp behind the College of William and Mary by a Safety Committee that is afraid he will use the army to make himself dictator. Less enemies than foils to each other, Dunmore's worst defect, bad judgment, underscores Henry's greatest virtue, intrepidity. The grudge match between good and evil fades to the spectacle of an "humane good man," as one loyalist termed Dunmore, laboring to turn himself into Washington's "monster."[1]

Having twice exploited the sottish ineptitude of the rebel leader Col. Hutchings at Kemp's Landing, Dunmore is inclined to "venture something" in a bloody fiasco at Great Bridge – only to compound his error at Gwynn's Island, a horror beyond even his powers of circumlocution. From time to time, the arch villain is replaced by the comic figure from Italian farce: Dunmore, sputtering with rage after being blown (or pushed) off his quarterdeck during a hurricane; Dunmore, lamenting that Virginians should think "I [had] nothing more at heart than the utter destruction of this once most flourishing country," when he had threatened to do nothing less; Dunmore, signing off from Virginia in July of 1776 in a stentorian ecstasy of rage, frustration and disgust:

"I have done!
DUNMORE

With this book, I end my account of Lord Dunmore as Governor of Virginia. For all his tomfoolery, I shall be sorry to see him go. Like acting Lt. Gov. William Nelson, left at the Palace door while Dunmore dallied in New York, I find that "I begin to like him."[2] He loved to play the *roué*; often, he was a boor, yet he could also be a kind and loyal friend. There are two things he was not: a drunk and a fool. The evidence for this is quite conclusive. Here is Lord Dunmore as he appeared in 1781 to James Boswell, one of the most entertaining writers in the English language:

THURSDAY 8 JULY
... I was to dine with Major Montgomerie at the [officers'] mess at Fortune's [tavern]. I went up to him ... [at Edinburgh] Castle before dinner; drank some excellent porter, which set me a-going. Walked down [the hill] with him to

the mess and drank so heartily there that I was quite intox-
icated. It was a very hot day. I went to the [regimental] roll-
calling at night on the Castle Hill, and talked a great deal
to many people. I did not recollect one word that I said.
But Mr. Lawrie [a solicitor] told me that Lord Dunmore
and I took off our hats to one another and bowed very
often. So we had been very complimentative. His Lordship had dined at the mess, but was sober. I asked him and
Sir James Campbell and Sir John Paterson of Eccles to sup
with me, and I went home to give notice. They all came,
but by that time I was so ill that I was obliged to go to bed.
My valuable spouse behaved admirably, had supper prepared, and pressed them to stay. But they did not.[3]

As might be expected, Boswell awoke

in sad distress and in great vexation at what had happened
last night. I was very grateful to my wife and said she was
worth a million. After being a little in the Court of
Session,* I waited on my three last night's guests. Sir
James Campbell was ill and confined, but the other two
very obligingly supped with me this night, as did Mr.
Nairne [another barrister] and Miss Susie Dunlop. We
were quite sober. Lord Dunmore did not drink one glass
out. He talked very well.

Like Augustine Prevost before him, Boswell found Dunmore
not only able to handle his liquor, but exceedingly courteous,
even allowing himself to be drawn into a silly round of
hat-doffing with a drunk.

Fifteen months later, a "high-spirited" but soberer Boswell
dined with Dunmore *en famille*, where he was introduced to

---

* The supreme court of Scotland where Boswell, a barrister, had most of
his practice.

Lady Charlotte Dunmore and two of her three daughters, Lady Augusta and Lady Alexandra, whom Boswell described as "beautiful young creatures with Parisian vivacity and airs."[4] Having done the Grand Tour of Europe, with a stopover in Paris where he made a conquest of more than a few beautiful young creatures, Boswell was something of an authority on vivacity. He was also, thanks to his intimate connections with the *literati* of London and Edinburgh, as able to recognize intelligent conversation as any man in the English-speaking world. That the author of the life of the brilliant conversationalist and wit, Dr. Samuel Johnson, by all accounts the greatest biography ever written, found Lord Dunmore to be a good talker is no small thing.

Interestingly, the tavern where Boswell intended to dine on July 8, Fortune's, was also the meeting place of Lord Dunmore's favorite Edinburgh social club, the Poker Club. The name of the club was derived from its symbol, a poker, reflecting the members' predilection for stirring the fires of controversy by taking a "poke" at the British government's policy toward Scotland. As the Poker Club included the cream of Scotland's intelligentsia, that would not have been difficult. David Hume, the philosopher, was a member, as was the historian James Robertson, economist Adam Smith, law lord Baron Grant and the "intellectual lords" Dunmore, Marischal and Elibank. The club also had many lawyer members, all ornaments of the bar, many destined for the bench. So far were the Club's afternoon dinners from being drunken routs that we are informed that "a close attendant . . . never observed even an approach to inebriety in any of the members."[5] Another source describes Fortune's tavern as enjoying the "highest vogue" among Edinburgh's society:

The gay men of rank, the scholarly and philosophical, the

common citizens, all flocked hither; and the royal commissioner for the General Assembly held its levees here, and hence proceeded to church with his cortege, then additionally splendid from having ladies walking in it with their court dresses, as well as gentlemen.[6]

It is clear that Dunmore enjoyed the company of great minds as well as fine women and that, to borrow a phrase from Helen Maxwell, a rebel lady from Norfolk, he was well used to free and facetious conversation. Clearly, he liked his jokes, and if the butt of the joke was someone important, so much the better. In this category we may place the following story, circulated by Dunmore after getting it from the Duchess of Gordon. It seems that Lord Cornwallis of Yorktown fame, having heard rumors of madness in the Gordon line, objected to the marriage of his son to the Duchess's daughter, Louisa. Hearing of this, the Duchess demanded a *tête à tête*, in which she told him, "I know your reason for disapproving of your son's marriage with my daughter: now I will tell you one thing plainly, – *there is not a drop of the Gordon blood in Louisa's body.*"[7] Thus relieved of his fear of madness in the family by this assurance of his future daughter-in-law's illegitimacy, Cornwallis withdrew his objection.

It is true that the taint of immoral, or at least imprudent behavior dogged Dunmore throughout his life. Most of this was his own fault, but not all of it and not the worst of it. The worst, which occurred in 1793 while he was serving as Governor of the Bahamas, was the unlawful marriage of his daughter Augusta to the King's son, Prince Frederick Augustus. The marriage was annulled, and though George III would later agree to give Augusta an annuity, proper British society never forgave Dunmore, his Lady or their daughters for the transgression. Here, a young society girl anticipates encountering Lady Dunmore and her disreputable daughters at a party:

> Tomorrow we are going to a party where we are to meet everybody, for you must know that even in this small society there is an improper set. Lady Dunmore and her daughters, Lady Virginia Murray, and the married one, Lady Susan Drew, sisters to the Duchess of Sussex* . . . are visited by very few proper people, but [their] . . . houses are the rendezvous of officers.[8]

At the time of the party, Lady Dunmore was about 70.** She was only 54 and trying to keep up appearances "with the aid of rouge" when Gouverneur Morris, The American Minister Plenipotentiary to France, came across her at the Haymarket Theater in 1792, but the effect of faded elegance, if not decadence, was already there:

> In the Box adjoining to us is Lady Dunmore and family. With the Aid of Rouge she looks I think as well as when I saw her in America nearly twenty years ago, and then she was pretty well advanced and rather to be admired for Grace than Beauty.[9]

In short, if Dunmore in his final portraits seems sour-faced, it may be because he had cause. A subject of ridicule for leaving his post in Virginia, embarrassed by the conduct of his family, (conduct which he had angrily defended to the King himself), he was more to be pitied than scorned. To be sure, he seems a comic figure at times, but he was never the caricature that Virginians claimed. Like Patrick Henry, he tried to bring on a war; like Henry, he succeeded, only to find that the war had passed him by.

* Lady Augusta's adopted title.
** The exact date of Lady Dunmore's birth is unknown.

Which brings us to the perennial question overhanging this revolution. Was it about British tyranny or giving vent, as Edmund Randolph put it, to "a hasty feeling?" Once again, we are obliged to note that no one in America enjoyed more liberty than a white Virginia planter. This is not to say, of course, that Virginians had nothing to complain about, or that they did not have good reasons, political as well as ideological, for seeking independence from Great Britain. That said, one is tempted to suggest that in 18th Century Virginia, liberty meant the right to overreact and that Lord Dunmore's principal role in the affair was to model the vices that leant dignity to the histrionics.

Perhaps we spend too much time trying to find external causes for this revolution. Certainly that is how it seemed to Edmund Burke, whose speech on the "true temper of [American] minds," delivered in Parliament on May 22, 1775, should be required reading for anyone who seeks to understand Virginia and the period:

> There is, however, a circumstance attending these colonies, which in my opinion, fully counterbalances this difference [in religious beliefs] and makes the spirit of liberty still more high and haughty than in those [Americans] to the northward. It is, that in Virginia and the Carolinas they have a vast multitude of slaves. Where this is the case, in any part of the world, those who are free, are by far, the most proud and jealous of their freedom. Freedom is to them not only an enjoyment, but a kind of rank and a privilege . . . I do not mean, Sir, to commend the superior morality of this sentiment, which has at least as much pride as virtue in it; but I cannot alter the nature of man. The fact is so; and these people of the southern colonies are much more strongly, and with a higher and more stubborn spirit, attached to liberty, than those to the northward . . . In such

a people the haughtiness of domination combines with the spirit of freedom, fortifies it, and renders it invincible.[10]

Burke was not saying that there was a "good side" to slavery, or that the Revolution was a put-up job. Nor did he mean to discount the role of agitators and propagandists on both sides of the Atlantic. His point, rather, was that in the slave-owning southern colonies, particularly Virginia, extreme pride and fear of the loss of freedom were deeply rooted in the mental and physical landscape. That the high and haughty spirit of the Virginians could be tamed by Parliament was absurd. Human nature was against it, and whatever might be said about prospects for future reconciliation, the wisest and best course for the government would be to acknowledge and accept the inevitable.

The war would go on, and a lengthy, bloody and destructive war it would be. Lord Dunmore and a clumsy, tyrannical government would be blamed for having lit the fuse. But the truth is, the American desire for freedom was bred in the bone for reasons both good and bad, and no one was more in touch with that desire than the planters of Virginia. That is why, when the war was over, it was the Virginians who were asked to draft the new republic's founding documents, thereby ensuring that slavery would be as much a part of the country's future as it was its past.

War!

Believe me, Sir, the unlucky step of calling that gentle-
man [Patrick Henry] from our councils where he was
useful, into the field in an important station, the duties of
which he must in the nature of things, be an entire
stranger to, has given me many an anxious and uneasy
moment.[11]

Edmund Pendleton to William Woodford Jr.,
December 24, 1775

George Mason, a highly-regarded planter from Virginia's
Northern Neck, told George Washington that the Third
Virginia Convention, which began sitting in July of 1775, made
him sick. He meant it literally: "I hinted to you in my last [let-
ter] the parties and factions which prevailed at Richmond. I
never was in so disagreeable a situation, and almost despaired
of a cause which I saw so ill conducted. – Mere vexation and
disgust threw me into such an ill state of health, that before the
convention rose, I was sometimes near fainting in the House.
Since my return home, I have had a severe fit of sickness, from
which I am now recovering but am still very weak and low."[12]

Edmund Randolph would later say of Mason that he saw
"[a]t a glance to the bottom of every proposition."[13] That was
just fine for thinking and writing, but it left little room for
negotiation and compromise, or as Mason put it, "undoing one
day, what [was done] . . . the day before":

I have not since I came to this place, except the fast-day and Sunday, had an hour which I could call my own. The committee (of which I am a member) appointed to prepare an ordinance for raising an armed force for the defence and protection of this colony, meet every morning at seven o'clock, sit till the Convention meets, which seldom rises before five in the afternoon, and immediately after dinner and a little refreshment sits again till nine or ten at night. This is hard duty, and yet we have hitherto made but little progress, and I think shall not be able to bring in the ordinance till late next week, if then. This will not be wondered at when the extent and importance of the business before us is reflected on – to raise forces for immediate service – to new model the whole militia – to render about one-fifth of it fit for the field at the shortest warning – to melt down all the volunteer and independent companies into this great establishment – to provide arms, ammunition, &c., – and to point out ways and means of raising money, these are difficulties indeed! Besides tempering the powers of a Committee of Safety to superintend the execution. Such are the great outlines of the plans in contemplation.[14]

Mason did not say so, but much of the chaos in Richmond had to do with Virginia having been placed in a state of rebellion by Lord Dunmore's sudden departure. His Lordship's many provocations notwithstanding, few Convention delegates wanted war.[15] This is not to say that they doubted the need for an army; but an army meant a commander in chief, and why did that have to be Patrick Henry, a man so totally ignorant of the arts of war – though if the issue was fighting spirit, who was better qualified than Henry? But Henry was a force of nature, and dealing with a force of nature while you are melting down volunteers and molding them into an army would be hard for any colonial assembly, let alone one placed in a state of rebellion.[16] Not until August 9 – twenty-three days after the start of the Convention – was Patrick Henry finally able to get away from the Second Continental Congress and return to Richmond. With him came three other Virginia delegates, bringing with them all their fears at the prospect of Henry as Commander in Chief: Edmund Pendleton, Thomas Jefferson and Benjamin Harrison.

Edmund Pendleton
"Bringing his fears at the prospect of
Patrick Henry as
Commander in Chief"

Whether Henry was upset to find the Third Convention in a state verging on anarchy is unknown. But there is no doubt that he joined other delegates in asking the Convention President, Peyton Randolph, to resign on the 16th of August: Randolph was ill, and the request was unanimous. While no one could have known that his growing debility and recurrent episodes of confusion would end two months later in a "sudden palsey" at the home of a Philadelphia wine merchant, there was general agreement that managing the chaos in Richmond was too much for him.[17] In short, though the arrival of Henry added to the confusion, it also gave the Convention a much-needed focus.

Patrick Henry was not surprised to find his name put forward for the position of Virginia Commander in Chief. He had asked for the job. Pendleton, who had stunned John Adams by being the only Virginian to vote against Washington as Commander in Chief of the American Army, now astonished many Convention delegates by not opposing Henry for Colonel of the First Regiment, a title thought to carry with it automatic appointment to the position of Commander in Chief.[18]

To be sure, by the time Pendleton arrived in Richmond the decision was largely a *fait accompli*. It is also the case that Pendleton's calculus was always very nimble in any matter involving Henry. In a June 1775 letter to French and Indian War veteran William Woodford, Pendleton had said, "[I] did not mean when I spoke of the dissensions about Mr. Henry's Manouvre [at Doncastle's Ordinary] to hint at blaming our Committee [of Safety], or the probability of division among them, they took the right method of commending the Zeal and good intention of the Party tho' they disapproved the Measure."[19] In alluding to Henry as "the Party," Pendleton was revealing characteristic discretion. Private letters had been known to fall into the wrong hands before, and even oblique criticism of a demagogue could be dangerous in a time when legislators were trying to new model the militia. Meanwhile, the Party himself, alert as always to the mood of his audience, was proposing that the issue of what was to be done with the gunpowder purchased with the money he had extorted from "Old Corbin," (Richard Corbin), the King's Receiver of Quitrents, be laid before the Convention for disposition.[20] Viewed merely as a political tactic – "old Corbin" was one of Pendleton's friends – this was wise; viewed as a gesture intended to appeal to back country delegates, it was a stroke of genius, though the Convention as a whole elected to leave the issue to Virginia's congressional delegation. Meanwhile Pendleton, probably with encouragement from Woodford, had come to a decision of his own.

William Woodford
"Invited to exercise the powers of a Commander in Chief"

Even before he became Chairman of the Committee of Safety, Pendleton had had "anxious and uneasy moments" over the thought of Patrick Henry at the head of an army.[21] Part of this uneasiness had to do with the belief that Henry was simply unqualified for the job, and part with the memory of Henry's 1765 call for a Cromwell to stand up for America, which Pendleton's father-in-law, Speaker John Robinson, had denounced as "treason."[22] Nor was Pendleton likely to forget Henry's ridicule of the former Speaker's loan office proposal – or his advocacy in support of the inquiry that exposed Robinson's practice of loaning the colony's retired currency to bankrupt planters. With his snowy hair and courtly manners (Henry used to say Pendleton had "too much courtesy"), Pendleton belonged to another era – Robinson's era – with its patronage and its political intrigue.[23] Robinson's patronage had shaped Edmund Pendleton's career, both as a lawyer and as a legislator. Now the deftest political operator in Virginia, Pendleton specialized in parliamentary obstructions so counter-revolutionary that, according to Phillip Mazzei, he was called "Moderation Pendleton."[24] As Pendleton put it in a December 24, 1775 letter to Woodford, Henry's election to the position of Commander in Chief was a mistake which could not be remedied because he had done "nothing worthy of degradation and must keep his rank."[25] Pendleton would see that Henry kept his rank – knowing that his rank could be used to keep him. Meanwhile, Henry's second in command, Woodford, was to be ordered into the field and invited to exercise powers that his Commander in Chief, left languishing at the capital, could only enjoy in theory.

Woodford was never Pendleton's creature. But he did hope, as a supposedly tried and true veteran officer, to become a beneficiary of his patron's dislike for Patrick Henry. If nothing else, Woodford could model the case against inexperienced and impetuous leadership. Best of all, Woodford was "prudent," an epithet applied so often to him by Pendleton that it might be described as "Homeric," except that what Pendleton had in mind was the very opposite of heroic. What the term signified for Pendleton was pliability, "follow-ship" and loyalty to one's patron. Woodford had all the old values, amongst which an instinct for the main chance ranked very high. To suggest that Pendleton's interest in Woodford was limited merely to cultivating him as the non-Henry alternative would however be going too far. The men were friends, as the affectionate tone of Pendleton's letters to Woodford would suggest. That said, there can be no doubt that in making an ally of Woodford, Pendleton was beginning the process of neutralizing his Commander in Chief. This was to be an alliance founded on the fear of Henry. Its only constraint was a reciprocal want of candor.

By contrast, the dispute between Henry and Pendleton was open and forthright. Patrick Henry wanted war. Pendleton wanted only a "redress of grievances, not a revolution." For Pendleton, the old colonial House of Burgesses was merely in adjournment. If the Convention was not illegal *per se*, it was verging on usurpation in its encroachment on Crown prerogatives. Pendleton believed that delegates could enact no laws, only ordinances bearing "the face of law" – though every ordinance, according to George Mason, followed all the formalities of law-making. No one, not even Convention President Randolph himself, was to be granted executive powers. The kind of decisiveness Henry had put on display at Doncastle's Ordinary was to be shunned for process. Every issue had its own committee, with the Assembly acting as a Committee of the Whole. The "Committee on the State of the Colony," populated by some of the Convention's best talkers – men like Richard Bland, Robert Carter Nicholas, George Mason, Carter Braxton, Thomas Nelson and a newly-radicalized James

Mercer – was so large it included a fourth of the delegates. After Dunmore, the gravest threat to Virginia was its increasingly dysfunctional government.[26]

But while George Mason was being sickened by all the chaos and confusion, Pendleton was delighting in its opaqueness, as a general might delight in cannon smoke on a battlefield. When the vote for Commander in Chief was finally taken, it was found that Patrick Henry had been elected by just one vote – and that by a plurality – over his closest rival, Thomas Nelson, Jr. Even the most avid Henryite had to admit that this was something less than a vote of confidence. Having assumed jurisdiction over Henry's Military Commission as Chairman of the Safety Committee, Pendleton was now able to do what he could never have done by opposing Henry's election directly: use his skill with "resolutions, reports and laws" to make sure that Col. Henry never took the field.[27]

At first glance, Henry's Commission seems to be all blather and boilerplate. In fact, it is a work of art: clear in its limitations, lawyer-like in its overlapping ambiguities. Subject to the order of the Convention, Henry was to be given command of all Virginia forces. And what if the Convention was not in session? Henry would answer to the Committee of Safety. And if the Committee was not in session? Then he would answer to its Chairman, Pendleton, empowered by Henry's own Commission to exact "obedience to all [his] orders and instructions."[28] Since army officers were also barred from serving as Convention delegates, Pendleton would have little to fear from Henry's oratory. If the Commander in Chief had a complaint, he could tell it to Pendleton.

When the Convention ended on August 26, Henry set out at once for Scotchtown. It took him a month to put all his affairs in order. By September 21 he was back in the capital. The next day, he drew his first paycheck from the Treasurer: it was £75 for two months. He then issued his first order: the First Virginia Regiment was to report to Adj. Gen. Bullitt at the Capitol. As an order, it barely signified; as *prima facie* evidence of Henry's new status it merely added to Pendleton's cascading anxieties.

Henry then followed up with an order establishing a system of military discipline. This was not only proper; it was essential. For want of discipline, the militia had gotten used (according to the *Gazette*) to waiting on anyone who had "uttered expressions highly degrading to the good people" of Virginia and escorting them back to their camp at Waller's Grove for trial. The indignities on offer for the guilty included the compliment of a fine "coat of thickset," being "drummed through the city" and forced to give "public Concessions" – the latter to be reported *verbatim* in the *Gazette*. It all sounded like so much clean fun, except that it was meant to be strike fear into the hearts of anyone who "sport[ed] with the great and glorious cause of America" and "thickset"* was a South Carolina euphemism for a skin-searing coat of tar and feathers.[29]

But if the new Commander in Chief's first acts were militarily appropriate and sensible, the Safety Committee's orders to Henry were overly abrupt, verging on the plainly insulting. "In Committee at Williamsburg October 3, 1775: Ordered that the Commanding Officer of the Regulars direct the building so many century [sentry] boxes as he thinks Necessary for the Centinels posted as a Guard to the Magazine." It was signed "Jno. Pendleton, Junr., Clk."[30] Henry would become inured to getting his orders from Pendleton's twenty-something nephew. But even assuming that he was innocent of the arts of war, directing him to appoint sentries and limiting his discretion to the number and placement of their boxes was not only

---

* A fustian-like cotton cloth.

inconsistent with the respect due a Commander in Chief, it threatened to turn a Colonel into a Sergeant of the Guard. By contrast, the Committee's October 24 directive, ordering Woodford and his men into the field and "repos[ing] great confidence in [his] judgment and discretion" found it "unnecessary . . . to point out the particulars of [his] conduct," except to suggest that he use his "usual prudence."³¹ Other, subtler indignities were to follow: In his orders, Henry was always addressed as "Sir," while Woodford's orders, some of them written by Chairman Pendleton himself, were directed to "My Dear Sir." If not exactly fond, the Committee's orders to Woodford were always cordial and never abrupt. Even a dull man – and Henry was never that – would have sensed distaste, if not distrust. Yet he remained patient, even passive. He was always correct, certainly never impetuous. But if Henry's failure to insist on the dignities due a Commander in Chief surprised his enemies, it positively mystified his men, who before long were seen to be meeting (according to John Page) "irregularly," and "without [Henry's] presence . . . as a mark of their Suspicion of [the Committee's] Judgement."³²

The orator who had been so quick to call for a Cromwell for George III was proving oddly slow in reacting to the war waged against his authority by Pendleton and Woodford. Before long, the void of his diffidence would be filled with increasingly broad orders to his rival. Thus, while Henry was counting sentry boxes at the Powder Magazine in Williamsburg, Woodford was being encouraged to move "towards Norfolk." Henry would retain his impressive title, but the honor of facing the enemy would go to Woodford. There it would stay. Never again would Patrick Henry get close enough to Lord Dunmore to bully him.

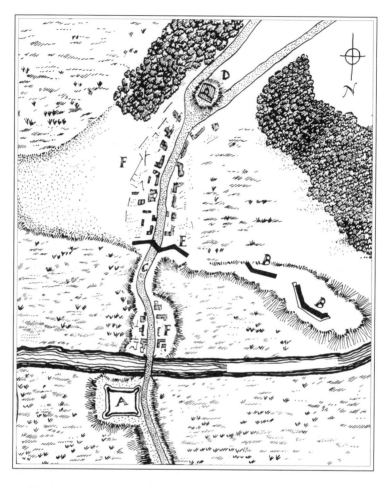

Lord Rawdon's Map (redrawn) Illustrating the Battle of Great Bridge.
Key: A. Fort Murray (the Hogpen); B. Rebel Entrenchments; C. The Causeway;
D. The Church and the Main Rebel Encampment; E. The Rebel Redoubt;
F. Houses in the Town of Great Bridge.

The Battle of Great Bridge

While Pendleton trifled with Henry, Dunmore was amassing an army and a fleet. The total number of loyalists and escaped slaves who flocked to him after his elopement is unknown, but it was ultimately enough to populate two regiment-sized units of 150 to 200 men each, the "Queen's Own Loyal Virginians" and the grandly-described "Lord Dunmore's Ethiopians." On August 1, he received the first 60 of what would ultimately number 134 grenadiers of the 14th Regiment of Foot, sent to him from Florida by British Commander in Chief, Gen. Thomas Gage. Meanwhile, he had added three British warships to his armada of armed tenders and pilot boats: the 14-gun sloop *Otter*, captained by Matthew Squire; the 16-gun sloop *Kingfisher*, captained by James Montagu and the 20-gun *Mercury*, captained by John McCartney. The 20-gun man-of-war *Fowey* having returned to Boston in July, Dunmore had moved his flag – along with 13 field pieces – to the pressed Jamaican merchant ship *William*. He was still seeking cannons for the Norfolk merchantman *Eilbeck*, seized by him in mid-July. All in all, it was an impressive force, both sea and land, growing more so by the day – a circumstance that did not go unnoticed by George Washington, who warned from Boston that if Dunmore was "not crushed before spring he will become the most formidable enemy America has."[33]

Meanwhile, nature was taking a hand. A storm, described as the "worst within the memory of man" by the *Norfolk Intelligencer*, struck Lord Dunmore and his fleet on August 29. John Pinckney (of Pinckney's *Virginia Gazette*) declared the storm the worst in Virginia history, adding that the damage to crops was "inexpressible," with the corn "laid level with the ground." Having chosen his Norfolk anchorage for its relative safety, Dunmore was surprised to find himself blown off his quarterdeck and severely ducked owing to some "confusion [among his] sailors." While his "dirty ship captains" (as Pendleton called them) were fighting to save their own ships, Dunmore was being fished, spitting mad, out of the Elizabeth River by his poker-faced sailors. Capt. McCartney did manage at great effort to keep the *Mercury* from foundering, only to find, come sunrise, that it was resting on a sandbar within range of a unit of Culpeper riflemen. Meanwhile Capt. Squire, who had been up the Elizabeth River on a sheep-stealing expedition, was forced to abandon ship, making a gift of it and all its stores to the rebels.[34]

Dunmore did his best to dignify his war with nature in his next report to London. As usual, his choice of words – and conspicuous omissions – opened a window to his soul. He noted Capt. Squire's "narrow escape," but failed to mention the kindness of Thomas Finn of Hampton, who had offered Squire shelter in his home after finding him clinging to a tree in the storm.[35]

This was war and Dunmore might be excused for overlooking Finn's kindness to Capt. Squire. But perhaps not for failing to note that Squire's stores, for which Dunmore was now demanding satisfaction from the rebels, had been returned to the captain's crew by Finn as a present. Exactly what Squire used for a disguise and how he obtained a canoe from "some Negro" so he could paddle back to Norfolk seemed to be beyond even Dunmore's powers of description. In his letter to Lord Dartmouth, Capt. Squire was portrayed as the victim of "a violent gale," a would-be marauder blown so far off course as to be obliged to take to the woods to avoid being "thrown into gaol." "We have demanded satisfaction of the people at Hampton for the sloop [wrote Dunmore] and desired that the

King's stores might be returned, to all which they have given us a positive refusal: their port is now blocked up and we have taken two of their boats and shall not permit a vessel to pass or repass until they have returned the stores, etc. They have called to their assistance between two and three hundred of their shirt men *alias* rebels." The childish sarcasm of "shirt men *alias* rebels" was perhaps typical of the Governor who could at one minute amaze a Shawnee Chief by leaping like a boy, while viewing Virginians' normal political aspirations as personal betrayal at the next.

The same impulses were evident in Dunmore's account of two earlier expeditions. The first involved a raid planned and organized by himself but actually commanded by Capt. Squire. The target of this, according to Dunmore, was the presses of the *Norfolk Intelligencer,* guilty of "aspersing . . . his majesty's servants . . . in the most scurrilous, false and scandalous manner."[36] "The public prints of this dirty little borough of Norfolk [he added] has [*sic*] for some time past been wholly employed in exciting in the minds of all ranks of people the spirit of sedition and rebellion." (Naturally, he failed to note that the subject of the *Intelligencer's* scurrility was himself.) The exploit of Williamsburg stocking-maker Adam Allen, solicited by his Lordship to steal the Great Seal and Crest of Virginia from the Capitol office of Secretary Thomas Nelson Sr., seemed at first to be in the tradition of the prankster Governor of New York, as described by Col. Richard Bland.* But unlike his assault on Chief Justice Horsmanden's coach and six, this exploit had a purpose: the theft of the Great Seal was meant to strip the rebel government of its claim of legitimacy.

---

* For the story of Dunmore's pranks as Governor of New York, see George Morrow, *A Cock and Bull for Kitty* (Williamsburg, Va., 2011)

The 14th Regiment's successful raid on Kemp's Landing ("Kemp's I"), planned by Dunmore but led by its commander, Capt. Samuel Leslie, presumably offered weightier fare. Yet Dunmore's account of his role in the raid seemed oddly self-effacing. The question was, why? That he wanted to show Dartmouth that he was not (as he said) "altogether inactive" was clear. What was not so clear was how much the developing conflict in Virginia was a hostage to his fear of being rebuked.[37]

In fact, it would be six months before Dunmore got another letter from Dartmouth. What he described on June 25, 1775 as impatience for "orders for my future governance" was to become by December 6 desperation over not receiving "one syllable . . . for these six months." "I have prayed and entreated your lordship over and over again for instructions," he complained, while admitting to "agreeable surprise" at the sudden arrival of Dartmouth's dispatches Nos. 21–23. As we will see, he had good reason to downplay his "little knowledge of military operations" – perhaps even to insist, as he now did, that "if he had done wrong, blame must not be laid at my door." That said, his account of an abandoned and bewildered Dunmore rang true: "God only knows what I have suffered since my first embarking from my anxiety of mind, not knowing how to act in innumerable instances that occur every day, being one moment diffident of my own judgment (and not having one living soul to advise with) and then on the other hand fearing, if I remained a tame spectator and permitted the rebels to proceed without any interruption, that they would by persuasion, threats, and every other art in their power, delude many of His Majesty's well disposed subjects to their party."[38]

Dunmore knew that he was ignorant of the arts of war; knew that he lacked judgment. In his eponymous war against the Shawnee he had been inept but lucky; now he was in danger of seeming merely incompetent. On the 17th of October, he was given an opportunity to show that he was neither inept nor a spectator: in the morning, he received intelligence of a large cache of rebel gunpowder at Kemps Landing; by noon he had Capt. Leslie and his 14th Regiment sailing down the Elizabeth River's South Branch. A few hours later, and Leslie had disembarked and quick-marched to within two miles of town. Though he had been told that there were 400 rebels in the neighborhood, and though his line of march took him through a dense forest at night, Leslie continued on to Kemps Landing. There he found the town deserted and the powder gone, the effect no doubt of a timely warning. After pillaging a few houses, Leslie marched his men back through the same dense forest, apparently as oblivious to the possibility of a rebel ambush going as he had been in coming. How much of his behavior was inspired by Dunmore's anxieties over becoming a tame spectator and how much by Leslie's own fears of inaction, the sources, unfortunately, fail to say.

For all his efforts to affect the self-effacing hero, Dunmore could not be Dunmore without crowing a little over Leslie's triumph: "I can assure your lordship [he told Dartmouth in his next letter] that landing in this manner discouraged exceedingly the rebels and raised the spirits of the friends of government so much that they are offering their services from all quarters." It was not unusual for Dunmore to sing the praises of a dutiful subordinate. And he did so now. As the head of his Lordship's little corps, Leslie received one of his chief's handsomest posies: "I should do manifest injustice to our little corps if I did not inform your lordship that upon all these occasions both officers and soldiers behaved with that order and spirit that does them honor."[39]

In fact, neither Dunmore nor Capt. Leslie knew how close to disaster they had come. The 400-odd rebels said to be in the area had indeed been warned that the British were on their way. Some of the men, recalling the tactics used at Lexington and Concord, pleaded to be allowed to lay an ambush. Instead, they were sent home on the excuse that the British had come from an unexpected direction. Two other units, totaling 70 men, all of them located within a mile of town, were dispersed after it was reported that a local planter had offered to point out their hiding place to the British. The rebel commanding officer, Col. Joseph Hutchinson, a burgess from Norfolk, then made so free with the bottle that he passed out in a field.[40] There he was found by a kindly butcher who, in an effort to spare him the indignity of arrest, buried him under two cart-loads of garbage. When he heard of this later, Pendleton was reported to have sighed for the "bleeding Hon[o]r of Virginia."[41]

Pendleton still had faith in a redress of grievances from the King. He called Dunmore "Wronghead," as if the former governor were no worse than the sum of the errors of his ways.[42] At the same time, Pendleton was alarmed to read intercepted letters from Norfolk's "Scotchmen . . . to their friends in Britain exaggerating the exploits of Lord Dunmore" and claiming that the Virginians were poltroons, no more adept at war than "the unhappy People of Princess Ann and Norfolk."[43] It was thus not for defensive reasons alone that Pendleton in September ordered George Nicholas and a company of the 2nd Virginia Regiment to march to Hampton to repel the insults of Capt. Squire.[44] As the *Otter* continued to inflict insults, Pendleton decided on October 24 to put the rest of the 2nd Regiment on alert, reinforcing it with five companies of Culpeper minutemen. He then ordered Woodford to march to the vicinity of Norfolk to cut off British sources of supply, though Woodford was told not to bring on a general engagement.[45] The next night, October 25, one of Squire's raiding parties landed a few miles east of Hampton and looted a number of houses. The following morning, the Captain himself, in a large schooner accompanied by a sloop and three tenders, appeared off the mouth of the Hampton River and threatened "to set fire to the Town."[46] The stage was set for the first battle of the war in Virginia. All that was missing was Virginia's Commander in Chief.

Col. Henry remained in Williamsburg, presumably to attend to the city's defense. Meanwhile, Col. Woodford was being encouraged by Pendleton to call in aid "any companies of minute-men or militia, which the exigency of affairs may, in your judgment, render necessary."[47] (Should he do so, he merely had to give notice to the Committee and his Commanding Officer.) As always, prudence was to be Woodford's watchword: a thrice-repeated caution on how he "protect[ed] and defend[ed] . . . friends to the cause of America" and a twice-stated condition to actions "offensive or defensive." The order to provide "intelligence by express, from time to time, to the Committee . . . and the commanding Officer here, of such things as to you shall appear necessary" was also stated twice. Initialed by seven of the Committee's eleven members, Woodford's orders ran to a verbose 800 words. Even Washington – Woodford's kinsman and mentor – would have puzzled over orders like these. Were they in fact orders or merely the record of an ongoing debate within the Safety Committee? Was he being sent to Hampton to make war or to reconnoiter, report and await new instructions? Woodford would have been hard put to say. What he could say, if he were being honest, was that his orders left him with something he did not want and could not use, discretion, while his rival, thought to covet it too much, was left with details as remote from the business of war as he was from the battlefield itself.

Henry's orders kept him out of harm's way; they also kept

him out of Woodford's.[48] He would have no share in any of the blame; but neither would he share in the glory. Henry's first orders, a note of 100 words, instructed him to procure a wagon and dispatch it to Lester's Ferry (a crossing on the James River south of Richmond) to pick up a load of gunpowder. His second, a mere 21 words, wished that he would tell one Mr. Hanson, "at his peril," not to go to Norfolk. In neither case did Pendleton make reference to his orders to Woodford or to Woodford's rules of engagement, issues on which his Commander in Chief might be expected to have something to say. Nor did Pendleton mention that he had detached 600 more riflemen from Henry's own 1st Regiment. (Only after the fact, on October 25, did Pendleton finally inform Henry as to what he had done, sending him a copy of the Committee's resolution for forming an encampment near Norfolk.) The fact that time was of the essence might excuse haste, informality and even an abrupt tone. But it did not excuse leaving the Commander in Chief in the dark as to the disposition of his own forces, the Safety Committee's plan of attack or their view of the role he was expected to play in the ensuing action. Nor did it explain why he was being asked to issue "necessary orders for the . . . execution" of a plan which he had never seen and in which he was to have no part. Yet, somehow, Henry bore it all, even an abrupt directive to avoid "unnecessary delay."

Squire's threat to burn Hampton was meant to secure the return of his lost stores. A more immediate reason for it might have been his frustration at the gall of the Hampton Safety Committee in ordering boats sunk in the channel to keep the *Otter* from entering the harbor. While his men attempted to clear a passage, Squire stood off from shore and cannonaded the town. By nine o'clock p.m., word of his actions had reached Pendleton and his Committee. This time, there was no hesitation. Col. Woodford was ordered to take Capt. Abraham Buford ("an experienced and brave officer") and 100 Culpeper riflemen and go at once to Hampton.[49] There he was to take command of all forces in the area and mount a vigorous counter-attack, making use of the war camp set up by Henry at Norfolk.[50]

Woodford did manage to reach Hampton by eight a.m., but only after a night ride through a torrential rainstorm while carrying all of his supplies. He found Capt. Squire still in the channel. The cannons on his schooner, war sloop and three tenders continued to fire but to little effect, thanks to the marksmanship of the Culpeper riflemen, among whom was the fourth great grandfather of the writer of this little history.* Able to kill at great distances, the Culpeper men made climbing the rigging to sight the cannons suicide. Squire, who seems to have belonged to the "my men failed me" school of officer, would later say that his problems at Hampton were the result of his men's reluctance to stand by their guns. Modesty apparently forbade him to mention his own sudden departure at the height of the battle – an act so impressive to the captain of one of the British tenders that he promptly jumped overboard and swam as fast as he could for shore, leaving behind a crew of "five white men, a woman [and] two slaves," as well as "6 swivel [gun]s, 7 muskets . . . a sword, pistols, and several papers." What a woman was doing aboard the *Hawke*, Pinckney (from whose *Gazette* this account is taken) failed to say.[51]

Aside from a few broken windows and a splintered door panel, the town of Hampton was unscathed. It was hardly a

---

* "[The riflemen are] remarkably stout and hardy men; many of them exceeding six feet in height. They are dressed in white frocks, or rifle-shirts, and round hats. These men are remarkable for the accuracy of their aim; striking a mark with great certainty at two hundred yards distance." James Thacher, M.D. *Military Journal of the American Revolution, 1775–1783* (Gansevoort, N.Y., 1998), p.31.

battle. But if it was hardly a battle, it was a great victory for Virginia. For a week, the toast in the capital's 30-odd taverns was "Woodford, Nicholas and Buford!" Having had nothing to read about for weeks but Squire's pillagings, Virginians were ecstatic. A letter in Pinckney's *Gazette* called the Hampton affair "proof of [Virginians'] natural bravery." Pinckney's *Gazette* extolled the army's "spirit and bravery,"[52] while wishing for "another skirmish." Another letter writer warned Squire to "take care," Virginia riflemen could kill at *400 yards*.[53] Pendleton told Richard Henry Lee that Dunmore was so frightened at the accuracy of the Culpeper men's rifled guns that he had ordered the sides of every ship in this fleet "caulked up above men's heights."[54]

The effect of the rebel triumph at Hampton on Dunmore was predictable. It made him furious; or rather, it made him more insistent than ever on not becoming a tame spectator. He lacked judgment; he had none of the attributes of a leader, but his Lordship was no coward. His fear, always, was that he would be found wanting; his remedy, increasingly frenetic action.

At the beginning of October, Dunmore had told Dartmouth that "a very small force well applied now . . . would soon reduce the whole of this southern part of His Majesty's continent to a proper state of submission. I do beg and entreat your lordship that I may not long remain an inactive spectator."[55] To be sure, his war had yet to achieve the desired effect: instead of reducing cities to ashes, he had pillaged houses; instead of suppressing a rebellion, he had inspired new contempt. An example of the latter, according to Pendleton, was the recent "droll contest" over a cider boat. It began at Burwell's Ferry with a rifleman scaring off the war sloop *Kingfisher* with a single shot. (The fatal accuracy of which was immediately confirmed by the shrieking of a British regular.) It ended – after a daylong pursuit – with the seizure of the now empty cider boat at Jamestown. Capt. McCartney's fury at the accuracy of the Culpeper riflemen, the absurd disproportion in the size of the two vessels and the futility of the contest were all, for Pendleton, Wronghead personified – and by the way, had Jefferson (his correspondent) heard that Lord Dunmore "daily expects to be recalled?"[56]

Virginians knew that Dunmore would read their letters in the *Virginia Gazette*; knew how keenly he would feel their ridicule of his ship captains' clumsy efforts at war-making. What they may not have known was how fiercely determined he was to give better than he got. It was his system of justice, his code of laws: insults, more than good deeds, had to be repaid. And what better way to repay the insults and scorn of his tormentors than to take personal revenge on them in the very place, Kemp's Landing, where Virginia's honor lay bleeding only a month before? So it happened that on November 15, 1775, his Lordship found himself at the head of a detachment of the 14th Regiment of Foot marching through the same dense forest that had nearly spelled disaster for Capt. Leslie. Helen Maxwell described the inglorious outcome:

[In the fall of 1775] . . . Lord Dunmore took it into his head to make an excursion into the country, at the head of his troops, consisting of a fine body of grenadiers, and a large company of refugees, and carried all before him. A number of the militia, indeed, from Norfolk, and all about commanded by Col. [Hutchings] . . . had been drawn up in a field [at] Kempsville to stop the march, but when they saw the British coming, with colors flying, army shining and drums beating, they all took to their heels and ran away as fast as their horses and legs could carry them, without staying to fire a single shot. I saw them myself racing off at a fine rate through Kempsville . . . [rebel Capt.] Matthews among them, whipping up his horse and crying out as loud as he could bawl to 'Take care of the powder! Take care of the powder!' The Colonel, however, being full of Dutch courage stayed behind and not being in a condition to keep up with him, fell into the hands of the enemy and I heard some of the British officers laugh and say that they had taken him lying flat on his back in the field, and crying out, 'We'll die in the bed of honor!,' though they added, that he was already dead – dead drunk, at least. After this, Lord Dunmore entered the town in triumph, at the head of his soldiers and proceeded at once to establish his headquarters at Mrs. Logan's. Here he erected his Majesty's standard, and those who could not conveniently run away went at once and took the oath of allegiance. . . . Never, I suppose, since wars began, was there a victory more complete or won with so little loss of blood.[57]

This time Col. Hutchings *had* laid an ambush; he had even dismounted and joined his men on the firing line, a bit of bravado that failed to change the result but at least showed fighting spirit. Unfortunately, at the first sight of a red coat, a green volunteer had let off a shot. Dunmore reacted with confusion, which Hutchings might have exploited had he been in command of his senses. Instead, he became his Lordship's captive, a result that might have been far more unpleasant than it was had Dunmore not decided to send him to Boston to be held for a subsequent exchange of prisoners. Nine days later, Dunmore was feted by the people of Portsmouth with a parade featuring Capt. Leslie's grenadiers, rolling drums and a fine flurry of flags.

For Norfolk's beleaguered Scots, Dunmore was now man of

the hour: protector, military chief. He had set aside the Governor in favor of a more exalted character: "a humane good man."[58] Meanwhile, his army was growing quickly: "not less than three thousand," Dunmore told Gen. Howe in November, "had I but a few more men I would march immediately to Williamsburg."[59] Escaped slaves also continued to come to him – though less than 400 could be considered fit for duty. One loyalist thought Dunmore's "humanity appeared in a conspicuous light, as he could easily have surrounded & cut off the [the rebels at Kemp's II] but he was satisfied with taking some prisoners."[60] Another assured his brother in London that "L. Dunmore is so much admired in this part of the County That he might have 500 Vollunteers to march with him to any part of Virginia."[61]

Kemp's II was to be the high water mark of Lord Dunmore's war with Virginia. Like Abraham Lincoln, who would rely on Gen. McClellan's 1862 victory at Antietam for political and moral authority to issue his Emancipation Proclamation, Dunmore had been waiting for a victory to help him recruit an army of avenging slaves. That he hoped to produce consternation is clear. What is not so clear, amid all the Virginians' jokes about "our African friend," is whether he intended the far-reaching moral, social and political implications of his act.

It was enough for his purposes that slaves flocked; that Virginia's economy should be paralyzed; and that his regiments of Ethiopians would help him reduce Virginia and its cities to ashes. Nor is it accurate to say that he was the first to think of inciting a slave insurrection. But it is hard to believe that with his love of practical jokes and his insight into human nature he did not see the irony – and the rhetorical advantage – of unleashing Virginia's slaves to avenge the wrongs done to them by masters who claimed to be "slaves of Great Britain."

Dunmore's Proclamation of November 7, 1775, issued on board the *William* off Norfolk, offered to turn Virginia's so-called "revolution" inside out. It declared "all indented servants, Negroes, or others, (appertaining to rebels) free that are able and willing to bear arms." Never mind that his power as the self-deposed Governor of Virginia stopped short of freeing the slaves of anyone – let alone casting doubt on the propriety of the British government's support for the highly lucrative slave trade. Never mind that requiring "every person capable of bearing arms" to join his army "or be looked upon as traitors" used the color of law (the King's standard) to achieve what Parliament had yet to decide: that Britain was formally at war with Virginia. For all that, Dunmore's Emancipation Proclamation – the first such proclamation to be issued in America – deserves to be better known. Here it is, in all its blustering glory:

A PROCLAMATION

As I have ever entertained hopes that an accommodation might have taken place between Great Britain and this colony, without being compelled by my duty to this most disagreeable but now absolutely necessary step, rendered so by a body of armed men, unlawfully assembled, firing on His Majesty's tenders, and the furnishing of an army, and that army now on their march to attack His Majesty's troops and destroy the well disposed subjects of this colony. To defeat such treasonable purposes, and that all such traitors, and their abettors, may be brought to justice, and that the peace, and good order of this colony may again be restored, which the ordinary course of the civil law is unable to effect; I have thought fit to issue this my Proclamation, hereby declaring, that until the aforesaid good purposes can be obtained, I do in virtue of the power and authority to me given, by His Majesty, determine to execute martial law, and cause the same to be executed throughout this colony: and to the end that peace and good order may the sooner be offered, I do require every person capable of bearing arms, to resort to His Majesty's STANDARD or be looked upon as traitors to His Majesty's Crown and Government, and thereby become liable to the penalty the law inflicts upon such offenses; such as forfeiture of life, confiscation of lands, etc., etc. And I do hereby further declare all indented servants, Negroes, or others, (appertaining to rebels) free that are able and willing to bear arms, they joining His Majesty's troops as soon as may be, for the more speedily reducing this colony to a proper sense of their duty, to His Majesty's Crown and Dignity. I do further order, and require, all His Majesty's Liege Subjects, to retain their quitrents, or any other taxes due or that may become due, in their own custody, till such time as peace may be again restored to this at present most unhappy country, or demanded of them for their former salutary purposes, by officers properly authorized to receive the same.

GIVEN under my hand on board the ship William, off Norfolk, the 7th day of November, in the sixteenth year of His Majesty's Reign [1775].[62]

Perhaps the most telling indication of the epochal character of Lord Dunmore's Emancipation Proclamation is that it provoked what can only be called elemental ferocity from the Virginians. In a resolution drafted on behalf of the planters of Richmond County, Landon Carter called it the product of "an entirely debauch'd mind an[d] [bo]dy now run mad with its own grinding iniquities and disappointments." He added "We do . . . most seriously conceive, that if this said John Earl of

Dunmore should b[e] permitted to exist any longer on any american earth, that during such an existence he ought to be placed securely chained to some MAD HOUSE, the only true security to his Majesty's *crown* and *dignity*."[63]

Though Dunmore was unable to judge the effect of Carter's capitalized fury first hand, the suasive power of his proclamation (and recent triumphs) was abundantly clear from the many people, black and white, who agreed to take his oath. One ardent loyalist described the men pouring into his Lordship's camp as "bees to the hive."[64] Robert Shedden, a Portsmouth importer, wrote his brother in London that he expected Dunmore to raise "such a party here as the shirt men dare not face." Yet another loyalist described a landscape literally muddied by artisans and farmers "stampeding" to escape the Committee of Safety's order that all able-bodied men serve in the Virginia militia. Neil Jamieson of the Norfolk merchants Norton and Sons was so carried away that he asked the home office for £5,000 worth of goods, to be ready for sale as soon his Lordship restored the peace.[65]

Indeed, for Dunmore himself, the days immediately after Kemp's II were a time of rare joy, marked by fetes and celebrations of his military prowess and jocular asides to patriots like Helen Maxwell whose complaint about the insolence of one of his Lordship's Ethiopians produced this amusing exchange:

'Why, Madam,' said [Dunmore], 'this is a provoking piece of insolence, indeed, but there is no keeping these black rascals within bounds. It was but the other day that one of them undertook to personate Capt. Squire . . . But pray, Madam,' continued he, 'where is your husband all this time?'

'Indeed, my Lord,' said I, 'I cannot tell you where he is . . .'

'But you will see him soon?' said he.

'I cannot say when I shall see him.'

'Well, Madam, when you do, you must be sure and tell him for me that this no time for a man like him to be out of the way. His Majesty wants his service and I will give him any place he will name if he will come in and join us. But join us he must.'

Shortly afterwards, I rose to go home, when his Lordship followed me to the door and, offering me his arm, insisted on seeing me safe to my lodgings.

I tried to decline the honor, especially as I thought there was some risk, saying, 'Oh! Don't trouble yourself, my Lord. It is but a step – and besides, I am afraid there is danger by the way, as some of our men may be lurking about and watching for a chance to shoot you.' (Though the truth is I was only afraid that they might miss their mark and shoot me.)

'Oh! As to that Madam, never fear – my sentries are all about, and I can't be caught napping.'

So I took his arm, and he escorted me very politely to Billy White's door*, where he bade me good night, but not till he had charged me again to be sure and tell Mr. Maxwell that he was very anxious to see him.[66]

Clearly, Helen Maxwell did not think of Lord Dunmore as a joke or a buffoon. On the contrary, she viewed him as a disarmingly subtle enemy who could deftly threaten her rebel husband in one breath and politely offer to see her safely home in another; a newly-vindicated military commander so sure of himself that he could not be caught napping; a satirist who found a moral in the insolence of "black rascals" refusing to stay "within bounds" – only to laugh it off with a racial joke

---

* A boarding house in Kemp's Landing

about a slave attempting to pass as a white British ship captain. A "jolly, good hearted" man with "coarse and depraved sensibilities"; an "unfit governor and military leader" who might yet become "America's greatest enemy"; a "humane good man" and "a monster"– all of these things were said about Lord Dunmore at one time or another, and all of them were true.

Had there been no sequel, had he not suffered a terrible reverse at Great Bridge, it is possible that Dunmore, not Lincoln, would be known as America's first Great Emancipator. As it was, he was forced to confront (and report) a disaster, for himself and for British prospects in Virginia. Thanks to the lack of British ships bound for London, Dunmore was given nearly three months to find a way to express the awful truth, only to find the awful truth inexpressible. Less a letter than a four-act drama of the mind, his eleven-page missive to Lord Dartmouth reveals a desperate man trying through revision to reconcile himself to a disaster, only to end by terming it "this little advantage."[67]

In fact, what Dunmore wanted to talk about was not the Battle of Great Bridge. It was himself. He began the letter by assuring Dartmouth that he was still "equipping a fleet, raising an army." By the time of the second installment, dated December 13, he had no need to talk about armies. His army was no more. The only question now was whether the blame would be laid at his door, or that of someone else. Left without instructions from London and "diffident of his own judgment," but with his spirits bouyed by his recent triumph at Kemp's II, it seemed that he had decided to "risk something" (as he put it) for the defense of his little fort at the town of Great Bridge:

> [I]t occurred to me that should I be able to prevail on only a few to espouse His Majesty's cause (with the very small force I had to support them), I should only involve them

in inevitable ruin, should the rebels march a body against us that we were not able to withstand. In this situation was my mind, when I was informed that a hundred and twenty or thirty North Carolina rebels had marched into the colony to a place called the Great Bridge.

If Dunmore's account was not much of a report, it was at least the true history of Lord Dunmore. Never had his own deficiencies intersected more directly with the impossibility of his situation; never would he work so hard to describe the state of his mind; never was he to find so little understanding or sympathy.

According to Dunmore, he had Great Bridge fortified on October 27, 1775. It was not until early December, however, that he learned that the rebels had procured cannons from North Carolina and were expecting further reinforcements from Williamsburg. "[K]nowing that our little fort was not in a condition to withstand anything heavier than musket shot," Dunmore explained, "I thought it advisable to risk something to save [it]." (Because, as always, his account of the event is as much the story as the event itself, it is quoted at length):

Captain Leslie, who commands the detachment of the 14th Regiment now here, marched on Friday the 8th . . . [of December] after dark from [Norfolk] to reinforce the garrison at the fort, with orders from me, if on his arrival there he found no material change, to order two companies of Negroes to make a detour and fall in behind the rebels a little before break of day in the morning and just as day began to break to fall upon the rear of the rebels, which I expected would draw their attention and make them leave the breastwork they had made near the fort. He was then, with the regulars, the volunteers and some recruits, to sally out of the fort and attack their breast-

45

work. He accordingly arrived at the fort in the night unperceived by the rebels. The Negroes by some mistake were sent out of the fort to guard a pass where it was thought the rebels might attempt to pass and where in fact some of them had crossed a night or two before, burnt a house or two, and returned. Captain Leslie, not finding the Negroes there, imprudently sallied out of the fort at the break of day in the morning. The rebels, as I suppose having got intelligence of this design, were prepared to receive him from behind their trenches and kept a very heavy fire upon them. Notwithstanding that, the advanced guard forced their way up to the breastwork, but being much weakened by the incessant fire of the enemy and discouraged by the loss of Captain Fordyce (who fell at the breastwork) were obliged to retire to the fort with the loss of three officers killed and 43 wounded . . . Captain Fordyce's bravery and good conduct (who fell with his hand on the breastwork) would do honor to any corps of any country: his loss is most sincerely lamented by all who knew him. Lieutenants Napier and Leslie [the nephew of Capt. Leslie], who were the other two officers that fell, were both very deserving young men and are really a loss to their corps. The greatest praise is due to both officers and soldiers of the 14th for the undaunted spirit they showed on this occasion.

Dartmouth had left him without a living soul to advise with, while Capt Leslie had failed to note a material change – which is to say, Dunmore hoped to divide the fault between the two of them. But it did not take a genius to see that a sally out of his fort, followed by a march under fire up a narrow causeway described by one observer as "one hundred and sixty yards [long]" was on the wrong side of crazy, even if, as Dunmore claimed, his black troops had been able to create a diversion.[68] Dunmore did go on to tell Dartmouth that the attack on the Rebel redoubt was entirely his own idea. His also offered explicit praise for the bravery and good conduct of Capt. Fordyce – while failing to note that it was he, Dunmore, who had sent poor Fordyce to his death by ordering him to lead the charge. With his insight into the hearts of men, Dunmore not only knew (as Helen Maxwell had put it) that Capt. Fordyce was "too good a soldier to flinch from any duty," he was counting on it.[69] What he was clearly not counting on was Fordyce's conviction that the attack could not succeed – a conviction so strong that, according to Helen Maxwell, he had given his watch and a message for his wife to a friend knowing that "he was going to his death."[70]

In his letter, Dunmore failed to accurately state the number of killed, wounded and captured. There was a reason for this. Of the 102 officers and men of the 14th Regiment present at Great Bridge, 81 were killed, wounded or captured. No wonder that the people of Norfolk were horrified. Like Helen Maxwell, they saw "the vehicles with the poor [soldiers] in them," being carted through town. They heard the wounded men cry "'Water, water!" Moved with pity, they brought vases of water, only to watch the soldiers drink with "a rabid thirst," which seemed "impossible to satisfy."[71]

Two days later, Capt. Leslie, what was left of the 14th and much of the population of Norfolk were loaded onto the ships and boats of Dunmore's little fleet. Having just lost his nephew, Leslie was in a mood to speak his mind. Never again, he wrote a friend in London, would he send men to die on a whim. He had known, sooner or later, that they would be "forced into some scrape."[72] This of course was no mere scrape. Yet, he and everyone else failed to put the blame on Dunmore. In his Lordship's army, action, even hasty, ill-considered action, was the order of the day: one had only to ask Capt. McCartney of HMS *Mercury,* placed in irons and sent off to Boston to be court-martialed for being too soft on the Virginians.

Still, in openly admitting the defects in his own judgment, Dunmore did manage to achieve an awkward dignity. Nor did he enact the part of a humane, good-hearted man only to friends. "I do assure your lordship [he told Dartmouth] it is a most melancholy sight to see the numbers of gentlemen of very large property and their ladies and whole families obliged to betake themselves on board of ships at this time of the year, hardly with the common necessaries of life, and great numbers of poor people without even these, who must have perished had I not been able to supply them with some flour which I purchased for his Majesty's service some time ago."[73] Kindness was not Dunmore's problem; judgment was. Faced with the bloody evidence of his bad judgment, he sought to change the subject to his foresight in buying flour to feed survivors and refugees. Perhaps it was best that he not dwell on the battle. Like the rebels, of whom he said their transitions from hope to despair were "very quick," he would get over it. In fact, he already had. What had initially caused him to "Rave . . . like [a] Mad Man," and "sw[ear] to Hang the Boy" who had told him there were only 300 men behind the rebel breastwork would henceforth be treated as merely an instance of Capt. Leslie's imprudence.[74]

Oddly enough, the view at the other end of the causeway was not all that different. Now forty, with his health impaired by the French and Indian War's rude toils, Col. William C. Woodford Jr. was known less for his record of success at arms than the peace he had negotiated with the Cherokees in 1762, for which a grateful House of Burgesses had awarded him a year's salary. Despite being pushed forward in Richmond by

Pendleton and others as the seasoned alternative to Patrick Henry, Woodford had only recently admitted to Gen. Washington that he suffered from inexperience. (The reply was cheering: his was a "common case" needing only "practice and close attention.")[75] Meanwhile – until practice could make him perfect – Woodford was under orders admonishing him in querulous italics, *"to risk the success of your arms as little as possible, at this important crisis."*[76]

Woodford arrived at Great Bridge on December 2. One look at the Hogpen, which Dunmore had said could not "withstand anything heavier than musket shot" was enough to remind Col. Woodford of his orders. Though he was expecting reinforcements from North Carolina, he immediately wrote to Pendleton asking for nine more companies of Virginia militia. They arrived five days later: six Culpeper rifle companies and three companies from Henry's depleted 1st Regiment, bringing with them enough powder and lead for an entire army. With 717 men in camp and 100 more en route, Woodford might have slept well the next four nights – had he not received the following express marked "Head Quarters" on December 6: "Not hearing of any dispatch from you for a long time, I can no longer forbear sending to know your situation and what has occurred . . . I wish to know your situation particularly, with that of the enemy, that the whole may be laid before the convention."[77] It was signed "P. Henry, Jun." At once, the enemy without was replaced in Woodford's mind by the irate enemy within, his much-neglected Commander in Chief. Woodford's reply, a letter so artful that it might stand as a model of its kind is dated the 7th of November.[78]

With Pendleton directing his every move, Woodford hoped he had little to fear. That said, it was quite true that until Monday, he had not written to Col. Henry "for a long time." Even then, he had not written to him directly, but only referred him to his letters to the Committee of Safety. To invoke the protection of the Safety Committee which had tolerated, if not abetted, his slights was one thing; to plead his case to an entire convention in front of the greatest orator who ever lived was quite another. In short, if it was true (as he said) that he could "not bear to be supposed to have neglected [his] duty" he must have slept rather badly on the night of December 8, as it was his duty – clearly stated in his commission from the Convention – to report from time to time to his Commander in Chief.[79]

Whatever the case, his fears of Henry were almost immediately replaced by revelations of war. Unknown to Woodford, most of Dunmore's 14th Regiment had slipped into the Hogpen overnight. The actual attack came at dawn. It was Adj. Gen. Bullitt who saw them first: two of Capt. Squire's gunners, wheeling their cannons into place at the causeway's south end in preparation for firing. Bullitt immediately shouted "Look out!" to the officer in command at the breastwork, Lt. Edward Travis, and sent a runner in search of Col. Woodford. Bullitt's runner reached Woodford just as an officer at the breastwork was heard to shout, "Boys, stand to your arms!"[80] That was enough for Woodford who "quickly pressed down to the breastwork" to have a look.[81] What he saw when he looked over the top of the rebel breastwork was no sight for a prudent man: there, gathered in front of the Hogpen, was an army almost the size of his own, including 102 grenadiers, men and officers, two regiments of Ethiopians and two of the Queen's Loyalists.

As Woodford looked on, the grenadiers fixed bayonets, formed a column six abreast and began to march up the narrow causeway leading into the town of Great Bridge. The Queen's Loyalists and the Ethiopians stayed back, apparently under orders to wait until the breastwork was taken. As he had been ordered, Capt. John Fordyce was at the front, leading the charge.

When the column entered the town, the rebel pickets took one last shot, stood up and ran back to the redoubt – all but Billy Flora, a free black man, who calmly continued to load and fire his rifle.[82] Finally, he too made for the redoubt, passing as he did over a crude plank bridge. Realizing that the grenadiers might have a use for that bridge, he then ran back and removed two of its planks – all this amid what one rebel participant described as a "shower of bullets."[83] With the British only 50 yards away, Lt. Travis ordered a general fire. Bullets (according to a British participant in the battle) began to whistle "on every side." Capt. Fordyce was not the first to be hit, but he was the first to fall, his knee shattered by a bullet. Somehow, he managed to get up. As bullets buzzed around him, he casually brushed his knee with his hand, a gesture one rebel said looked as if he were flicking away a very pesky fly. He then took off his hat, waved it, and in a feeble imitation of a victory cry yelled, "The day is ours!" Within seconds, he had 18 bullets in him. The attack collapsed. Those who still could ran away, followed quickly by the rebels, a few of whom stopped to help the wounded redcoats. Perhaps remembering a bracing Dunmore harangue on the rebel scalping practices, one of the grenadiers cried, "FOR GOD'S SAKE, DO NOT MURDER US!" The rebel, who was trying to drag the man to safety, said "Put your arm about my neck and I'll show you what I intend to do." The redcoat did as he was told and the two staggered to safety together.

The battle was not over. Dunmore had ordered a battery of cannons placed on a peninsula east of the causeway with the idea of using it to enfilade the anticipated American assault. A hundred Culpeper riflemen took it without a shot. They then turned their attention to the British reserve of loyalists and

Ethiopians, picking them off one by one until Leslie at last took mercy on them and ordered them back into the Hogpen. From a platform inside, Leslie watched as two of the shirt men "tenderly removed a wounded regular from the bridge." In a gesture peculiar to this, the first real battle of the war in Virginia, Leslie bowed his thanks.

Bullitt pleaded with Woodford to continue the fight. The sole casualty on the Rebel side was a single bullet-nipped finger, while British losses were all too obvious. Woodford refused. He was convinced – by the sheer, bloody insanity of the attack – that it was a feint. Later, one rebel, Capt. Richard Meade, would recall a "vast effusion of blood" on the causeway, "so dreadful that it beggars description": "a scene, when the dead and wounded were bro[ugh]t off, that was too much; I then saw the horrors of war in perfection, worse than can be imagined; 10 and 12 bullets thro[ugh] many; limbs broke in 2 or 3 places; brains turning out. Good God, what a sight!"[84]

Whether moved by pity or by relief, Col. Woodford was the first to propose a truce. His emissary told the British commander that he wanted time to remove the dead and wounded. Capt. Leslie, who had just witnessed the death agonies of his favorite nephew, was quick to agree, but by seven p.m. of that evening, he had decided to put no more trust in Woodford's compassion. He loaded what was left of the 14th Foot onto carts, quietly slipped out of the Hogpen and returned to Norfolk.

Though he heard the British leave, Woodford ordered no pursuit. He was busy with the gallant and brave Fordyce whom he interred with "military honors due to his great merit."[85] Seventeen of the British wounded were consigned to the tender ministrations of the surgeons. Six others, who might have died in the hands of the surgeons, had the good fortune to end up at the house of Polly Miller, the madam of Great Bridge, whose kindness on this occasion was destined to make her a great celebrity in her own lifetime (while adding to her custom).[86] One lightly-wounded British officer, Lt. John Batut, was so touched by the humanity of the rebel army that he insisted on sending Capt. Leslie a message under a flag of truce to tell him about it. (In his reply, Leslie expressed his sincere thanks, along with extreme sorrow for "poor Fordyce.")[87]

If by honoring Fordyce Woodford intended to flatter himself and his country with a show of civility, he succeeded.[88] John Banister, a delegate to the recently-convened Fourth Convention, could not refrain from writing to say how "sensibly touched" he was by Woodford's concern for his prisoners, a concern which "must do honor through your delicacy of sentiment to our national character."[89] A somewhat less dazzled Richard Kidder Meade declared simply that the British soldiers "fought, bled and died like Englishmen."[90]

In a letter to a friend written shortly after the battle, Woodford described it as a "Bunker Hill slaughter," adding "that there never was more execution done by fewer men."[91] Pinckney, in his *Gazette*, chose to stress the professional nature of the rebel battle preparations: "'there were only about 60 or 70 of our men at the breastwork; the rest were stationed at proper places and intervals, to cover them in case they had been forced from their entrenchments."[92] No one mentioned Woodford's failure to follow up on his victory – or Leslie's overnight escape. With 500 Highlanders rumored to be on en route, Woodford's "prudential system" (as one 19th century Virginia historian put it) received due, if reluctant support from his men.[93] Who cared about a few slaves or loyalists when they had just decimated a regiment of grenadiers? In fact, Woodford was as surprised by the result as anyone. He had not attacked Dunmore's fort. He had called for more reinforcements. He had not won a great victory. He had accepted one as a gift.

Five days later, the rebel army marched into Norfolk. They found it nearly deserted. Col. William Howe's North Carolinians having arrived on the 12th, there were now 1,275 of them: 350 of Woodford's 2nd Virginia Regiment, 172 of Col. Henry's 1st Regiment, 165 Culpeper riflemen, 438 regulars from Col. Howe's 2nd North Carolina Regiment and 150 North Carolina Volunteers.[94] After praising Woodford's gentility which, Howe said, "never forsakes him," and extolling his politeness (so "peculiar to himself"), Howe assumed the role of commander of the joint army.[95] The fact that he was Woodford's senior did not relieve Howe of the courtesies due a brother officer. Forgiveness toward his enemy was another matter. Thus, when Capt. Squire sent a flag of truce on December 16 to know if Col. Howe meant "to prevent the Navy & Army from being supplied with Provisions and Water," the answer was "yes," "to the utmost of our power."[96] Not only would the British get no fresh provisions, said Howe, he would do everything he could "to prevent . . . any communication whatever between the said Troops & Ships of War and this Town."[97]

For Howe, taking Norfolk was a mixed blessing: it was good to have the city in American hands, but the people, whom he called "disgraceful to Humanity, and worthy only of those who [are] lost to every sense of Publick Virtue or private Honour" seemed to him as undeserving as they were contemptible.[98] A Virginian, one Lt. Col. Scott, called the city a "most horrid place," "all the inhabitants on board the ships; flags [of truce] continually passing, asking water, provisions, or to exchange prisoners. Duty is harder than I ever saw before; our guards have not been relieved for 48 hours. The men of war fell down last evening about a mile, and left a brig with 5000 bushels of salt behind which our guard took, and brought to the wharf, but [we have] not got one bushel on shore yet." Those who stayed in the city were either thieves, British sympathizers or that blight on the tree of humanity: Scotsmen. Even as Woodford was writing his report to the Convention, he heard "some shots in the streets [and] three of our people wounded." "The town deserves no favor," he added ominously. The next day, he made the same point in another way: he had a local Scot, one Hamilton, "coupled to one of his Black Brothers with a pair of handcuffs . . . [to mark] the fate of all those cattle."[99]

It is unclear exactly when Cols. Howe and Woodford decided to destroy Norfolk. (Their contempt for its people had existed from the start; desire for revenge took a bit more time.) Two days after arriving in the city, they wrote a joint letter to Convention President Pendleton, advising him that the city should either be strongly fortified or "totally destroy'd."[100] Given the cost and time needed to build fortifications, the best option seemed to be the latter. But Norfolk was no Great Bridge, no dirty, ramshackle town inhabited by miserable wretches. Nor was it Williamsburg, a capital city of 1,500, which in Public Times swelled to six thousand. It was an important port, the second largest in Virginia after Alexandria: 10,000 souls residing in 1,500 homes, among them elegant townhomes that would grace the best addresses in Edinburgh and London, including the house of loyalist merchant James Parker. For Dunmore to raze Norfolk would be an atrocity; for a rebel army to do it, an act verging on the perverse.

St. Paul's Church, Norfolk
"His Lordship began a brisk nine-hour cannonade"

Yet, that was the case Howe tried to make in a December 22 letter to the Convention. Norfolk, he wrote, could not "be maintained with any troops you can place there, against an attack by sea & land, & if it could be maintained . . . your troops would be shut out from being any other way useful to you. . . . it must ever remain in the kind of war we are waging . . . dangerous to you."[101] This was at least partly true. But it would take a lot more persuading and, probably, a formal vote by the Convention before Virginians countenanced the destruction of Norfolk. There was a fear, expressed not only by British observers but many Americans, that the Revolution was fated to end – like the French Revolution 16 years later – in a reign of terror.

Happily, for every rebel error and atrocity, Dunmore was there to take the blame. On New Year's Day 1776, between three and four o'clock in the afternoon, his Lordship began a brisk nine-hour cannonade of Norfolk that threatened to do exactly what Howe had advised. What Howe did not say (in a letter written at ten that night) was that the cannonade was limited to houses along the city's wharves with the obvious intention of clearing them of rebel sharpshooters. Rather, Howe thought the wind "favor[ed] the design" and that "the flames *will become* general."[102] Was this a hint that the two commanders had decided to take advantage of Dunmore's cannonade to give effect to their own plan for dealing with the human detritus of Norfolk? For now, the Convention was left in the dark as to why Howe wished to laud "the bravery of our officers and men" in "hitherto" repelling such raids – and why their leaders had stationed them "in such a manner as will, we believe, render everything but burning the houses ineffectual."[103] Perhaps if the delegates had known what Howe knew (and as Dunmore would later report) that the wind that night was *off the land*, the question of who had done what might have been answered earlier.[104]

Whatever Woodford and Howe may have intended, there is no doubt as to the result. Speaking of the burning of Norfolk, one Virginia officer wrote, "The horror of the night exceeds description, and gives fresh occasion to lament the consequences of civil war. The Thunder of artillery, the crush of falling houses, the roar of devouring flames, added to the piteous moans and piercing shrieks of the few remaining wretched, ruined inhabitants, form the outlines of a picture too distressful to behold without a tear. I pray God I may never see the like again."[105] In 1777, a legislative inquiry found that 1,331 buildings were torched that night. The loss in property value was staggering: £176,426. The inquiry also found that of the 1,331 buildings destroyed in Norfolk, only 32 were burned in the British raid in November with an additional 19 destroyed in Dunmore's bombardment on New Year's night. Of the remaining 1,280 buildings, 863 were burned by rebel troops under the command of Cols. Howe and Woodford*.[106]

Norfolk's destruction was disclosed to Pendleton and the Convention on January 2 when Howe reported that parties of British soldiers had "landed & set fire to the Town in several places near the water tho' our men strove to prevent them all in their power but the houses near the water being chiefly of wood, they took fire immediately & the fire spread with amazing rapidity. It is now become general & the whole Town will I doubt not be consum'd in a day or two."[107] This, of course, was a lie; the town had been put to the torch by Americans acting under orders from Howe and Woodford. "Uneasy" at "having no Answer to [their letters] of the 1st & 2nd Inst," Woodford wrote again on January 5, this time to report that "nine tenths [of] the Town within the lines was consumed."[108] Why the fire had been allowed to burn until the entire city was consumed he did not explain, though what he did say – that the distillery of the Tory Andrew Sprowle was "Burnt . . . before we rec'd your [letter]" – was at least a tacit acknowledgement that he needed permission before he burned

* The others were ordered destroyed by the Convention to prevent their use by the British.

anything.[109] Nor is it surprising that Howe and Woodford were feeling uneasy, having just received the following letter from John Page, Vice President of the Committee of Safety:

> I think it would be better not to destroy the town, for it is possible that matters may be accommodated in a short time and in that case, we shall have done ourselves a great injury to no purpose and shall be laughed at by our enemies. It is true Norfolk may afford comfortable quarters to our enemy, but then destroying the houses will not prevent their repairing them, and building barracks, and we cannot prevent their keeping the port. Let them take the houses and let us confine them there, and cut off all communications between them and rest of the country. It may be the means of saving more valuable places. If our enemies oblige us to burn Norfolk, may they not oblige us to burn Portsmouth, Hampton and York?[110]

On January 6, uneasiness became panic with Howe writing Pendleton, "I have been waiting with an anxiety for the honor of an answer to the Letters of the first and second instant which I momentarily hope to be relieved of."[111] He then launched into a digression apparently meant to show that burning Sprowle's distillery somehow conformed to his orders, for if Sprowle's distillery deserved destruction, then perhaps so did Norfolk. "The town of Norfolk, Sir, is in a very ruinous condition, seven eighths of it being reduced to ashes, and tho' my heart bleeds for the suffering of individuals whose distress I truly deplore, yet I do consider it as to its ultimate tendency, as greatly beneficial to the public." How the ruin of Norfolk and the misery of its people could have an ultimate tendency greatly beneficial to the public being still somewhat unclear, Howe offered an additional justification: The people of

Norfolk, he said, "could [not] feel any strong prepossession in favour of America or its cause, [but were] suspicious friends therefore at best [who would retain] the power to become dangerous foes [were they] under the direction & protection of Government." The city was burned down not because it was overtly hostile but because it was filled with suspicious friends!

Then why deplore Norfolk's distress? And why call the burning "this accident?" The short answer is that Col. Howe was trying to put distance between himself and an atrocity. What followed was in the nature of a preemptive strike designed to avert blame for an atrocity by emphasizing his compassion for the victims: "I hope Sir I shall not have imputed to me a want of feeling for the . . . unfortunate Inhabitants of this Town, in the very moment that my mind is actuated by every painful sensibility which unavailable compassion can excite in a feeling bosom" – which is to say he now viewed the smoking ruins of Norfolk as a stage for the enactment of his better self. In fact, Howe's testimonial to himself was at odds with a "feeling bosom": rather than feel for Norfolk's misery, he preferred to deplore it with "*unavailable* compassion." Rather than pity his victims, he complained of his own "pained sensibility."[112]

Clearly, Howe was feeling a bit exposed. Only days before the burning of Norfolk, Sarah Smith, a resident, had asked him directly, apparently in the presence of Col. Woodford himself, whether he intended to burn down her house. "Yes," Howe was reported as saying, "I believe we shall burn up the two Counties" – meaning the counties of Princess Anne and Norfolk.[113] One Sgt. Henry Henly, a Norfolk man in Henry's 1st Regiment, later testified in the House of Delegates inquiry that on the night of the fire he was ordered to take a patrol to the waterfront where, to his great surprise, he found the fires from Dunmore's cannonade "in great measure *extinguished*."[114]

What he also found were rebel soldiers "with fire brands in their hands destroying . . . houses." William Goodchild, a Norfolk barber, told the inquiry that he had seen a rebel burning the privy of a prominent Norfolk merchant, probably one of the hated Scots. He asked the rebel if this was deliberate. "Yes, damn them, we'll burn them all!" was the reply.[115] Of course, alcohol played a part. Shortly before the fire began, Goodchild saw some rebel soldiers "roll a pipe* of wine out of the House of Capt. Cornelius Calvert and after beating in the head . . . dr[i]nk of the wine, & fill . . . their Canteens & bottles."[116] The fact that Capt. Calvert happened to be a good patriot and a former mayor apparently did not affect the soldiers' enjoyment of his wine.[117]

The only person who seemed willing to embrace the truth was Lord Dunmore. In the fourth, that is, February 13th installment of his four-part letter to Dartmouth, Dunmore noted that "The rebels, having burnt every house in the town (and many in the environs) of Norfolk, are retired to a village about ten miles from thence called Kemp's Landing. They have also ordered all the inhabitants of the two counties of Norfolk and Princess Anne to leave their habitations and retire to the backwoods. This and their many excesses, such as robbing, plundering and ravishing young women before their parents, has given great disgust as your lordship may easily believe to the unfortunate people in this part of the country."[118] Ravishing young women in front of their parents – if indeed it ever happened – was disgusting indeed. But the larger question in the war for public opinion would not be who ravished the girls of Norfolk but who razed their city. And the answer to that, as Dunmore knew, was almost certain to be himself. "As if," he sighed, "I [had] nothing more at heart than the utter destruction

---

* A large, lengthy barrel or cask with tapered ends.

of this once most flourishing country." Having seen how obligingly the rebels had set fire to the "part of the town . . . not in our reach," Lt. John Dalrymple, an officer in the 14th Regiment, had no illusions as to whom would be blamed. The rebels, he said, will take the "Inhumanity of the Action off their Shoulders" and put it "upon our own."[119]

Cols. Howe and Woodford had expected the Convention to accept their advice. The belief failing to sire the act, and the excuse of an accident seeming less plausible by the day, they decided to call all officers to a council of war in the hope of presenting a united front. Out of the united front then tumbled Col. Howe, burdened with the thankless task of going to Williamsburg for the purpose of "laying the state of affairs" before the Virginia Convention.[120] Exactly which state of affairs he was supposed to spread in front of the delegates was not clear. But if it was to be the truth, it would have to contend with "Huzzahs!" to the army and toasts "To the victor of Great Bridge!" How much easier to attribute the burning of Norfolk to Dunmore!

There are some lies which qualify as damn lies. Norfolk falls into that category. As Pendleton later told Woodford, "While the town was entire, I could not think it right for you to abandon it, as it was too shocking to think of our making a conflagration of our own town . . . *but after Lord Dunmore had done that horrid work, fit only for him, I saw no reason for your stay.*"[121] Evidently, Pendleton was referring to a state of affairs received from Howe's own mouth. The *Gazette* was even more willing to be convinced, discerning in Norfolk's burning not only proof of British cruelty but of the invincibility of American arms: "[We] can now glory in having received one of the keenest strokes of the enemy without flinching. They have done their worst, and to no other purpose than to harden our soldiers, and learn them to bear, without dismay, all the most formidable operations of a

war carried on by a powerful and cruel enemy; to no other purpose than to give the world specimens of British cruelty, and
American fortitude, unless it be to force us to lay aside that
childlike fondness for Britain, and that foolish dependence on
her we had borne so long."[122]

While Norfolk burned, Virginia's putative Commander in
Chief sat brooding, Achilles-like, in his headquarters' tent
behind William and Mary College. Though he had ample
grounds for complaint, Col. Henry had written Woodford a
rather cordial letter. Instead of peremptorily ordering him to
report to his Commander in Chief, as he might have done,
Henry styled his request for information as a favor to himself
to allay the "vast anxiety" of others. Instead of demanding an
explanation, he had asked about "the number and designs of
the enemy." He had even offered to help Woodford by deploy-
ing his own forces to create "some diversion."[123]

Having now received Woodford's reply, he was perhaps less
inclined to civility. Woodford's letter was disobedient; worse, it
was the kind of letter that Pendleton might have written: art-
fully-phrased and written in the knowledge that the Safety
Committee was on his side. Woodford claimed to be answerable
to Henry only when their two commands were joined. Quoting
directly from Henry's own military commission as Commander
in Chief, Woodford described his command as "a separate and
distinct body of troops, under the immediate instructions of the
committee of safety," or if the Committee was not sitting, the
Convention itself.[124] His only "indispensable duty" was to
report to these two supreme powers. Though nothing in his
orders relieved him of his duty to report to the Commander in
Chief, Woodford ended his letter with a dare that verged on
open defiance: "If I judge wrong, I hope [the Convention] will
set me right."

That Woodford was likely to get away with his insubordination Henry surely saw. As Pendleton's prudent friend, as the victor of Great Bridge, Woodford could now do no wrong. But there was more at stake here than his wounded pride and Woodford's indifference to military protocol. They both needed – Virginians needed – to know who was in command of their armed forces. With that in mind, Henry decided to lay the question before the Convention for a ruling. The Convention passed it on to the Committee of Safety which appointed one of its members, Joseph Jones, a lawyer trained at the English Inns of Court, to act as go-between. Jones' first act was to urge Henry "to treat the business with caution and temper as a difference at this critical moment between our troops wo[ul]d be attended with the most fatal Consequences." His second was to tell Woodford that Henry's Commission was more "strongly worded" than intended.[125] After a week of backing and filling, the Committee disposed of the issue by parsing it in half:

> Colonel Woodford, altho' acting upon separate or detached command, ought to correspond with Colonel Henry & make returns to him at proper times of the state & condition of the forces under his command, & to be subject to his orders, when the Convention or Committee of Safety are not sitting, but that whilst either of these bodies are sitting he ought to receive his orders from one of them.[126]

Apparently, Henry's career as Virginia's Commander in Chief was over before it had even started. The only question now was whether he would take his demotion quietly or lead another march on the Capital. The answer was neither. On February 28, Henry was called before the Safety Committee to be read a letter from Congress appointing him Colonel of

Virginia's 1st Regiment. That honor being already his and Congress having failed to accede to his request that he be named Major General over all six Virginia regiments, he decided to reject the appointment "without assigning any reason."[127] The next day, the Committee received his letter of resignation. Again, he refused to give a reason.

That the hero of Doncastle's had been grievously insulted was now clear to all. Henry might be willing to take his humiliation like a man, but his officers and men were not. They had come to fight. Nor did they much like being left sitting in camp as costumed window-dressing for a Commander in Chief who must never be allowed take the field against the enemy. Some of Henry's men had been with him since Doncastle's and admired him for his intrepidity. Others loved him for his easy amiability and indefatigable concern for his soldiers. "Honest Farmer," writing in Purdie's March 14 *Gazette*, went so far as to suggest that the neglect of Col. Henry had a motive: "[W]e apprehend that envy strove to bury in obscurity his martial talents. Fettered and confined, with only an empty title, the mere echo of authority, his superior abilities lay inactive, nor could [they] be exerted for his honor or his country's good." Whatever Pendleton might say in private asides to Col. Woodford about Henry's "Military Skill and discipline . . . appear[ing] more conspicuous since his departure," it was clear that more than a few Virginians believed that there was a plot to prevent Henry from ever appearing at the head of an army.[128] In any case, Henry's forbearance in the face of Pendleton's many slights – slights a would-be dictator would never have borne – spoke eloquently of his patriotism, his selfless sense of duty and his discretion.

On March 1, Purdie reported that six companies of "troops in this city being informed that Patrick Henry . . . commander in chief of the Virginia forces, was about to leave them, the whole went into deep mourning, and being under arms, waited on him at his lodgings."[129] The threat of a mutiny implied in Henry's men waiting on him under arms was about to become actual. More alarmingly, the threat seemed to derive much of its force and energy from the nominal Commander in Chief's own "spirited resentment to the [Committee's] most glaring indignities" – a point stressed by Henry's officers in the following address, which they had printed in Purdie's *Gazette*:

> Deeply impressed with a grateful sense of the obligations we lie under to you, for the polite, humane, and tender treatment manifested to us through the whole of your conduct, while we had the honor of being under your command, permit us to offer you our sincere thanks, as the only tribute we have in our power to pay to your real merits. Notwithstanding your withdrawing yourself from the service fills us with the most poignant sorrow, as it at once deprives us of our father and general; yet, as gentlemen, we are compelled to applaud your spirited resentment to the most glaring indignities. May your merit shine as conspicuous to the world in general as it hath done to us, and may Heaven shower its choicest blessings upon you.[130]

In his reply, also printed by Purdie, Henry thanked his officers for their approbation of his conduct, calling it an "ample reward for services much greater than those I had the honor to perform."[131] That afternoon, he was carried by his officers to the Raleigh Tavern for a banquet, enlivened by toasts to himself, Gen. Washington, the Continental Army and Congress. The stage was set for a riot.

While Henry's officers were chairing him around town, a few of his men, having assembled in what Purdie called "a tumultuous manner," were asserting their "unwillingness to serve under any other Commander." This assertion was followed by a demand for their discharge. Like it or not – and we have no sense that he did – Col. Henry was becoming the leader of an insurrection. He had a choice: he could live up to Pendleton's worst fears and appear at the head of a mob, or, as Honest Farmer said, he could use his superior abilities for his own honor and the good of the country. There was no question what he would do, only whether Virginians would await the outcome with patience.

It took the able assistance of his brother-in-law Col. Christian and a lot of personal capital, but by the following morning he had restored order. According to Purdie, Henry visited "the several barracks, and used . . . every argument in his power with the soldiery to lay aside their imprudent reso-lution, and to continue in the service."[132] Landon Carter, whose envy of Henry is well-documented, thought that the tale of Henry "harangu[ing] his mutinying soldiers" was merely "false praise" given to Henry by his friends and that but for [Adj. Gen. Bullitt] collar[ing] a man or two" and "clapp[ing them] . . . under a close confinement" there would have been no quiet for all of Henry's efforts.[133] While the fol-lowing testimonial, placed by ninety of Col. Woodford's officers in Purdie's March 1 *Gazette*, does not address that issue, it does suggest, albeit indirectly, that the anger in the army over the wrongs done to Henry was widespread: "whatever may have given rise to the indignity lately offered to you [the testimonial said], we join with the general voice of the people and think it our duty to make this public declaration of our high respect for your distinguished merit."

It is unlikely that Henry would have approved of the razing of Norfolk. While the record is discreetly silent as to what he said when he heard what had been done there, it speaks volumes as to his rectitude on every occasion on which it was put to the test. Howe's and Woodford's stated reasons for razing the city of Norfolk failed to meet the test of credibility. At best, their reasons sound like afterthoughts; at worst, they are belied by their oft-expressed wish to punish the inhabitants, particularly the hated Scots, of whom they had the worst opinion. Here was the usual justice of the victor to the helpless rendered under a cover of military necessity. Were it otherwise, it might have been disclosed to a candid world. But what would a candid world have said of burning a city of 1,100 homes because it was inhabited by "suspicious *friends?*"[134] As it happens, we have an answer to this question, supplied by Convention Vice President John Page, "we shall have done ourselves a great injury to no purpose, and shall be laughed at by our enemies."[135]

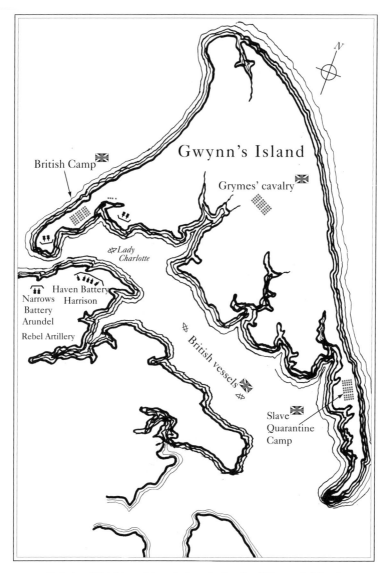

Rebel and British positions before the Battle of Gwynn's Island

The Battle of Gwynn's Island

It was now spring. The real war with Britain had yet to begin, while its proxy, Dunmore's vendetta, dragged on. Loath to abandon his Ethiopians and the many loyalists who had sought his protection, his Lordship was now sailing up and down the riverine byways of Chesapeake Bay, raiding farms and blasting away at the plantations of former members of his Council. Nor was there anyone to stop him. Col. Woodford was resting at home in Caroline County, while his co-commander at Great Bridge, now Brig. Gen. Robert Howe, was with Washington in New York. Their replacement, the whore-mongering, dog-loving British turncoat, Maj. Gen. Charles Lee, was off pursuing rumors of Sir Henry Clinton in North Carolina. Before he left, Lee had told Brig Gen. Andrew Lewis, whom he tasked with the defense of Williams-burg, that the plan was to deny Dunmore food, rest and water. It was hoped that eventually his Lordship would just leave Virginia.

The plan succeeded, but perhaps not in the way that Lewis and Lee had expected. On May 26, 1776 Dunmore put in for wood and water at Gwynn's Island on Chesapeake Bay. He found an abundance of both, including 200-odd cattle and sheep and over a 100 hogs. Some of the refugees on board the 80-plus vessels of his fleet had not had fresh meat for weeks. While they ate, Dunmore busied himself with organizing a mobile force, led by John Grymes, "the only [Virginian] of any consequence" (according to Dunmore) who had joined his army.[136] Meanwhile, another problem worsened. Though

Sir Henry Clinton
"Out of his
power to give any
assistance"

the recruiting of slaves was still going well, smallpox had "crept in amongst them [and] carried off a great many very fine fellows."[137] In Norfolk, Dunmore had ordered inoculations for anyone not immune to the disease, black or white, accelerating the process when he reached Gwynn's Island and was able to set up hospital tents. Still, it was clear that the situation on board the ships of his little fleet had gone from intolerable to desperate: ·

> [T]here were as many died almost as there were added to [the sick list, he told Germain]; in short, there was not a ship in the fleet that did not throw one, two, three, or more dead overboard every night. The Roebuck, I will venture to say, as well regulated and as clean a ship as any in the navy, had seventy-five on her sick list; and so in proportion had every other ship.

Like Great Bridge, the Battle of Gwynn's Island began at dawn, personally touched off by Brig. Gen. Andrew Lewis who had been dogging Lord Dunmore's ragtag fleet since January. The first rebel cannon ball smashed through the stern of his Lordship's flagship, the *Dunmore*, and travelled the entire length of the ship before finally coming to rest in the hold. With the rest of the rebel guns joining in, confusion was soon noted in the British camp.[138] Meanwhile Dunmore's pilot boats and tenders were busily scurrying out to sea. Not so the *Otter* and the *Dunmore*, which had to be laboriously towed out of range by long boats. Rebel reports to the contrary notwithstanding, British losses were minor: one dead and three seriously wounded. Though the *Dunmore* was reportedly raked fore and aft, the only injury suffered by his Lordship was to his ample thigh,[139] bruised by a splinter. "Good God that ever I should come to this!" he was heard to declare, though whether he was talking about dying in a dirty Virginia backwater or seeing all his fine furniture (stowed below decks on the *Dunmore*) smashed by rebel cannon balls was open to question.

By the next morning, all but one of the British warships had moved out of range. This was the *Lady Charlotte*, ungallantly abandoned by her crew after they ran her aground. Never one to miss an opportunity, Lewis promptly launched an armada of canoes and seized her. He then tried to land a force of 200 on the island. But it seems that he took too long to find transports for his men, with the result that most of the British soldiers left on the island escaped. It remained only to draw a moral lesson from the wretches left behind in a state almost beyond description:

> Many poor Negroes were found on the island dying of putrid fever; others dead in the open fields; a child was found sucking at the breast of its dead mother. In one place you might see a poor wretch half dead making signs for water, in another, others endeavoring to crawl away from the intolerable stench of dead bodies lying by their sides; in short it was a shocking scene.

Shocking enough, it was hoped, to discourage other slaves from joining his Lordship; shocking enough to make the practice of buying and selling human beings seem trivial by comparison.

In a July 15 letter to Thomas Jefferson, Safety Committee Vice President John Page wrote "2 more 15 Pounders & Powder & Ball in plenty we might have taken or utterly destroyed the *Dunmore*." If nothing else, Dunmore's "compleat drubbing" (as Page called it) meant that slavery could now be styled the lesser barbarity in comparison to the shocking scenes revealed on Gwynn's Island. This was war of course, and no one thought to ask why slaves should be so desperate for their liberty. It was enough that Virginia's moral authority had been restored and that Richard Henry Lee, soon to move the Congress for a declaration of independence, should be free to recur to the old jokes

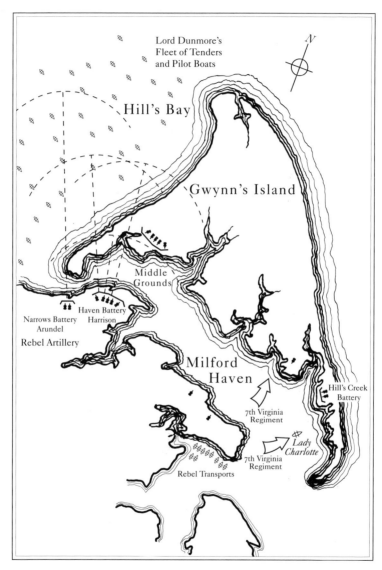

The Battle of Gwynn's Island

about Lord Dunmore: "we have no reason [he told Jefferson in July] to be sorry for the disgrace of our African Hero."

Meanwhile, our African Hero's fleet, which at one time had numbered 103 ships and barges, including five warships, was now reduced to a mere 40, with 20 of those bound for the West Indies. How he was serve the King without an army or a navy, Dunmore was at loss to say:

> [W]here we are to go, or what we can do next, to render service to his Majesty, I own I am puzzled to know, and I find there is now not even a chance of receiving any assistance. I really am at a loss what to determine on, for next month it will become very unsafe for the ships to keep the Bay, and I do declare I know not where we can go with our present force to make a harbour of any tolerable safety; for we no sooner appear off the land, than signals are made from it, when the coast is covered with men, and if we come to anchor within cannon-shot of either shore, guns are immediately brought to bear upon us, which it is not in the power of the ships to dislodge, as the shoals will not permit them to get near enough . . . I have taken the opportunity of advising all those who have put themselves under the protection of his Majesty's ships to proceed to such places of safety as they shall think proper. Some go immediately to Great Britain and others to St. Augustine.[140]

Even after being informed that it was "perfectly out of [Sir Henry Cinton's] power . . . to give him any sort of assistance," Dunmore refused to give up the fight:

> [This] will render my situation, if possible, more intolerable than it has been for these fourteen months past that I have been constantly penned up in a ship, hardly with

the common necessaries of life; but what makes it now a thousand times worse, is, that I am left without even the hopes of being able to render his Majesty the smallest service; this, I must say, is truly discouraging, and leaves me in the utmost difficulty to determine what to do.

In his final report from Virginia (quoted on page 70) he described how his once formidable army had been reduced to 108 "and those decreasing every day," as deaths from yellow fever and smallpox forced him to throw "one, two, three, or more " slaves overboard every night "from every ship in the fleet."[141] Our last view of him is from his quarterdeck, at the very moment of Gen. Clinton's arrival, when he learns that the British force of 1,000 men and six ships is intended for the Carolinas:

This moment General Clinton is arrived, and to my inexpressible mortification [I] find that he is ordered by your lordship to North Carolina, a most insignificant province, when this, . . . is the first colony on the continent both for its riches and power. Had North Carolina been your object, policy in my poor opinion ought to have induced your lordship to have ordered your army to have rendezvoused here for many reasons, first because this is a safe harbour both for access and riding in, where pilots are to be got, the other very difficult of access even for vessels of small burthen and not a pilot to be had, and when in, a very safe roadstead. Besides this, any little knowledge I have of military operations has ever induced me to think it prudent to conceal as long as possible your real intentions from your enemy. Which cannot happen here because it is impossible to expect that force coming from so many different quarters can all arrive at the same time or even near it; therefore, the enemy will have time to collect and prepare themselves.[142]

His admission of little knowledge of military operations was not wrung from him but freely offered. Soon, frustration would become terminal disappointment, signaled here by his recurrence to the word "mortification" and the phrase "total neglect": "To see my government thus totally neglected, I own is a mortification I was not prepared to meet with after being imprisoned on board a ship between eight and nine months, and now left without a hope of relief either to myself or the many unhappy friends of government that are now afloat suffering with me, but I have done." The letter was signed simply, "DUNMORE," in "large, bristling characters," that are so deeply incised on the historical record they could be called his epitaph.[143]

Dunmore the arch-fiend was gone. It was to be expected that the Virginians would celebrate. And so they did, while adding new dimensions of darkness to his Lordship's already blackened character:

Williamsburg, August 9th
By advices from Hampton, we learn that last Wednesday morning the Right Hon., the Earl of Dunmore . . . took leave of the capes of Virginia, where, he has, for more than a twelvemonth past, perpetrated crimes that would even have disgraced the noted pirate BLACK BEARD . . . So respectable a band will no doubt be a most valuable acquisition to the generals Howe and Clinton![144]

Meanwhile, Patrick Henry, governor since the 5th of July, was making himself at home in the Governor's Palace, sleeping in

75

his Lordship's bed and eating off his prize china. Nor was that the end of his insolence. Having been accused by Virginia "big-wigs . . . [of] being a coarse and common man . . . utterly destitute of dignity," he now went about in a scarlet cloak and dressed wig.[145] We are told that he "went to work with a will" and that he attended the Assembly on October 7; unfortunately, by the 30th, he was back home at Scotchtown, too sick to "attend to the duties of his office."[146]

Not until December 6 would Henry feel able to return to his office. Meanwhile, Pendleton, his Committee of Safety, Lt. Gov. Page and the Council were left to deal with the innumerable details of a state at war, not as a chief executive but as heads or members of ad hoc committees. In the five weeks that Henry was ill, Virginia endured three acting governors, the turnover of a third of the Council and the departure of the heads of its armed forces and the Continental Army's Southern Department. In addition, six of Virginia's nine regiments were sent by Congress to other theaters of war and the state treasury ran out of money. Elsewhere, the war in the north went from "half a war" (in John Adams' words) waged mainly against enemy lines of defense, to a war so one-sided that Washington's disastrous loss of New York was portrayed as a triumph of survival. By the time Gov. Henry recovered his health, America's Commander in Chief was literally running for his life.

Henry's first biographer, William Wirt, called 1776 "a dark . . . dispiriting period."[147] "[D]isheartened, and in want of every kind of comfort," Gen. Washington was said to be falling back "before an overwhelming power, which spread terror, desolation, and death, on every hand." This was the period of which Thomas Paine said "These are the times that try the souls of men! . . . For a short time the courage of the country fell . . . the heroism of the Virginia legislature gave way; and, in a season of despair the mad project of a dictator was seriously meditated."

Wirt had grave doubts as to whether Patrick Henry was involved in this mad project, Jefferson's insistence to the contrary notwithstanding. But was it the real Patrick Henry, the ghost of Tom Jefferson's malice or merely the left over aura of Henry's 1765 Stamp Act speech? Wirt could not be sure, though his tale of the encounter between an irate Archibald Cary and Henry's half brother Col. John Syme in the Assembly lobby has all the gloom and gathered portents of Shakespeare in the last act. "I am told [Cary said] that your brother wishes to be dictator; tell him from me, that the day of his appointment shall be the day of his death – for he shall feel my dagger in his heart before the sunset of that day."[148] Unsurprisingly, this threat caused "great agitation" in Col. Syme, who immediately assured Cary, "'that if such a project existed, his brother had no hand in it, for that nothing could be more foreign to him, than to countenance any office which could endanger, in the most distant manner, the liberties of his country.'" Wirt agreed. Those of Henry's friends he had interviewed all "finally and uniformly persisted in asserting his innocence."

Even the good wishes of Henry's old 1st Regiment were not above suspicion. In an address intended to hail his election as Governor of Virginia, they had characterized Henry as someone "[u]ninfluenced by private ambitions, regardless of sordid interest . . . [who not only] uniformly pursued the general good of your country [but] . . . taught the world, that an ingenuous love of the rights of mankind, an inflexible resolution, and a steady perseverance in the practice of every private and public virtue, lead directly to preferment, and give the best title to the honors of our uncorrupted and vigorous state."[149] In a brief effusion characterized by Wirt as "exquisite," Henry replied that however "*unmerited,* [and] *unsolicited*" his election, he intended to promote the "safety, dignity and happiness of the commonwealth." He closed with a salute to his soldiers, wistfully evoking the larger role he had once sought (and been promised) as Commander in Chief: "I honor your profession, I revere that patriotic virtue, which, in your conduct, hath produced cheerful obedience, exemplary courage and contempt of hardship and danger." Looking back over more than two centuries, it seems clear that Virginians were nearly as afraid of each other as they were of the British. The story of Cary's threat with its artful evocation of Julius Caesar and the Ides of March, signifies a feeling, not a fact – but one that seems no less powerful for being sourced in rumor and suspicion.

Within months, Virginians had gone from an idealism so pure that it left no room for compromise to a republicanism so fierce that they could imagine themselves as assassins of their fellow countrymen. Deprived by Lord Dunmore's elopement of a compelling reason for insurrection and ignored as a theater of war, they might have turned on each other had Henry not been as great a governor as he was an orator. In fact, the same attributes that made Henry an effective trial lawyer also made him a great executive: decisiveness, an instinct for the heartstrings of men and the vision of a leader. Perhaps his greatest virtue was his ability to admit deficiencies in himself. As he once said in reply to a critic of his ownership of slaves, "However culpable my Conduct, I will so far pay my devoir to Virtue, as to own the excellence & rectitude of her Precepts & to lament my want of Conformity to them."[150]

The rematch between Dunmore and the hero of Doncastle's Ordinary never came off. In the end, only Dunmore, the liar and presumed tyrant, was left to speak truth about Norfolk. He did so, first and most memorably, in his five-part letter to Lord Dartmouth.[151] He said that the city was razed by rebels; that he had ordered a few warehouses burned to eliminate them as places of cover, but "the wind . . . blowing off shore would have prevented the fire from reaching any farther." It was the rebels who had put the "finishing stroke to it by setting fire to every house." They had also "burnt many houses on both sides of the river, the property of individuals who have never taken any part in this contest. In short, from every transaction they appear to me to have nothing more at heart than the utter destruction of this once most flourishing country. Conscious I suppose that they cannot long enjoy it themselves, they wish to make it of as little use as possible to others." For once, his moral outrage rang true; for once, he was merely stating a fact. There was also a kind of awkward justice in the fact that it was he, in a lost January 18, 1776 issue of the *Gazette*, who first charged "Provincial Troops [with] burning the Town of Norfolk"; he who forced the Safety Committee to conduct a "Strict Inquiry."[152]

Dunmore arrived back in New York on August 19, 1776.[153] The following day he attended what was called a "great formal dinner," where he recounted his entire story to Gen. Howe and his officers. He must have done a good job, because he continued to dine with Howe and his staff daily for the next two months. Finally, on November 12, he sailed for London on the *Fowey*.

In 1781, he was returned to the House of Lords, where his most notable achievement was to serve as the butt for Edmund Burke's famous riposte to the claim that the army was holding the line in America. "Where is that?" Burke asked. "On board Lord Dunmore's ship?" Later, Burke extended the joke: "Neptune they say is to have a Pension, like Lord Dunmore for having lost his government." As he had in Virginia, Dunmore remained fiercely loyal to his friends, testifying on their behalf before the Royal Commission on the Losses and Services of American Loyalists, even as he was lobbying Lord Germain to secure the release of his friend Norfolk merchant James Parker. Nor did he fail to think of himself, demanding and getting

George Germain
"Lobbied by
Lord Dunmore "

£15,000 as a down payment on his losses in Virginia, in addition to £2,000 per year in lost salary along with a £1,000 *per annum* supplement. Still not done, in 1784 he filed a claim for £32,723 3s 2d, representing the value of furniture left behind in the Governor's Palace, his lodge on the York River, Porto Bello, a house and lot in Williamsburg, a farm in Berkeley County and 3,465 acres in Hampshire County (both now in West Virginia), along with the 51,000 acres on Lake Champlain he had purchased while Governor of New York. He got it all, less the £15,000 he had already been awarded. As historian John E. Selby put it, all that he lost in Virginia was his reputation.

He was not a moral man. But he did have a strong sense of loyalty to his friends. Even those who came to despise him – former friends like Capt. Foy and beneficiaries of his conscience payments like John Skey Eustace – agreed with that. He was not an honest man. But he was at least affable, energetic and, within limits, dutiful. No one asked him to stay on in Virginia; rather, Gen. Clinton's arrival was his clear signal to leave. But leaving would have meant abandoning all that had brought him to America in the first place, the hopes, as well as the emoluments that went with serving his king. With a few more warships, a larger army and better luck, he might have restored Virginia to the Crown. But the fault (as Hamlet says) was not in his stars. It was in him. If he had known that he was about to face disaster at Gwynn's Island, would he have left for New York after Great Bridge? It seems unlikely. He was no coward and he was persistent to a fault, continuing to exert himself for men like Capt. Foy and the Eustaces long after they had abandoned him. He never did have good judgment.

Notes

1   Neil Jamieson to Messrs. Glassford, Gordon, Monteath, & Co., Glasgow, 17 Nov. 1775 (an intercepted letter), *Revolutionary Virginia, The Road to Independence*, Robert L. Scribner and Brent Tarter, eds. (8 vols.; Charlottesville, Va., 1978), 4:425.

2   A paraphrase. Nelson's actual words were, "I think I discover many Good Qualities in him." See George Morrow, *A Cock and Bull for Kitty* (Williamsburg, 2011), p. 35.

3   Frederick A. Pottle, *Boswell, Laird of Auchinleck, 1778–1782*, (New York, 1977), pp. 118–119.

4   *Ibid.*, p. 263.

5   *Social Life in Scotland from Early to Recent Times*, Rev. Charles Rogers, ed., (3 vols.; Edinburgh, 1886), 2:373.

6   *Traditions of Edinburgh by Robert Chambers*, (New Edition; London, 1868), p. 178.

7   *Recollections of the Table Talk of Samuel Rogers, To Which Is Added Porsoniana*, William Maltby, ed. (New York, NY, 1856), p. 148.

8   *The Letter Bag of Lady Elizabeth Spencer-Stanhope, Compiled from the Cannon Hall Papers, 1806–1873*, A.M.W. Stirling, compiler (2 vols.; London, 1913) 1:144–145.

9   *A Diary of the French Revolution by Gouverneur Morris, 1752–1816, Minister to France During the Terror*, Beatrix Cary Davenport, ed. (2 vols.; Boston, 1939), 1: 179 and n.; see also *ibid.*, 1:185, 186 and 188.

10   *Edmund Burke's Speech on Conciliation with the American Colonies, Delivered in the House of Commons, March 22, 1775*, Wm. I. Crane, ed. (New York, NY, 1900), pp. 72, 75–76.

11   Edmund Pendleton to William Woodford, 24 Dec. 1775, *The Letters and Papers of Edmund Pendleton*, David John Mays, ed., (2 vols.; Charlottesville, Va., 1967), p. 141.

[12] George Mason to George Washington, 14 Oct. 1775, *The Life of George Mason, Including his Speeches, 1725–1792,* Kate Mason Rowland, ed., (2 vols.; New York, 1892), p. 210. (See also, George Mason to Martin Cockburn, 25 Aug. 1775, *ibid.,* pp. 203–204.

[13] Edmund Randolph, *History of Virginia* (Charlottesville, Va., 1970), p.192.

[14] *Life of George Mason,* 1: 201.

[15] See, for example, Lord Dunmore's "A Proclamation" of 7 Nov. 1775, on page 40 of this book.

[16] The story of the election of Virginia's first Commander in Chief is told briefly and well by the editors of *Revolutionary Virginia,* at 3:402, fn. 6, see also, George Mason to George Washington, 14 Oct. 1775, *Life of George Mason,* 1:210–212; George Mason to Martin Cockburn, 24 Jul.1775, *ibid.,* 1:200–202, "Narrative of John F. D. Smyth, 1769–1775" in *Travels in Virginia in Revolutionary Times,* Andrew J. Morrison, ed. (Lynchburg, Va., 1922), pp. 12–13.

[17] *Virginia Gazette* (Pinckney), 2 Nov. 1775.

[18] Pendleton would later claim that his failure to oppose Henry's election was consistent with "the Station [he] was honoured with" – i.e., Chairman of the Committee of Safety. Edmund Pendleton to William Woodford, Jr., 16 Mar.1776, *Pendleton Papers,* 1:159.

[19] Edmund Pendleton to William Woodford, Jr., 14 Jun. 1775, *ibid.,* 1:109.

[20] On Henry's proposal concerning the gunpowder, see Robert Wormeley Carter to Landon Carter, 10 Aug. 1775, *Sabine Hall Papers,* MSS Dept., Univ. of Va. Library.

[21] Edmund Pendleton to William Woodford, 24 Dec. 1775, *Pendleton Papers,* 1:141.

[22] For the story behind Henry's shocking speech, see George Morrow, *The Greatest Lawyer That Ever Lived* (Williamsburg, 2011).

[23] Quoted from "Judge Spencer Roane's Memorandum", George Morgan, *The True Patrick Henry,* (1907; reprt, Bridgewater, Va., 2000), 440.

[24] Phillip Mazzei, an Italian businessman drawn to Virginia in 1771 by the dream of making fine wine only to find himself swept up in a revolution, later wrote, "I felt it my duty to strip off his [Pendleton's] mask, for his doctrines could have undermined us. In every circumstance, he recommended 'Moderation,' so that if he had been able to influence the opinion of the people the English could have conquered us without

opposition . . . Men of clear vision called him 'Moderation' instead of Pendleton." "Memoirs of Phillip Mazzei," E. C. Branchi, trns., *The William and Mary Quarterly*, (Oct. 1929), 9:247–264, 249.

25 Edmund Pendleton to William Woodford, 24 Dec. 1775, *Pendleton Papers*, 1:141.

26 *Life of George Mason*, 1:252.

27 The other members of the Committee of Safety were: George Mason, John Page, Richard Bland, Thomas Ludwell Lee, Paul Carrington, Dudley Digges, William Cabell, Carter Braxton, John Tabb and James Mercer.

28 *Revolutionary Virginia*, 3:498. Henry's commission was approved "in form" by the Committee of Safety on August 26, 1775. The original parchment document, dated September 18, 1775, is lost.

29 *Virginia Gazette* (Pinckney) 7 Sep. 1775. As Pinckney noted, Joshua Hardcastle of Williamsburg was happy to be allowed "to give concessions" and nothing worse.

30 *Revolutionary Virginia*, 4:162.

31 *Ibid.*, 4:270–271.

32 Vice President John Page to Patrick Henry Esqr., 4 Nov. 1775, *Ibid.*, 4:321.

33 George Washington to Richard Henry Lee, 26 Dec. 1775, *The Writings of George Washington from the Original Manuscript Sources, 1732–1799*: Vol. 4. Electronic Text Center, University of Virginia Library, http://etext. virginia.edu/etcbin/toccernew2?id=WasFi04.xml&images=images/modeng&data=/texts/english/modeng/parsed&tag=public&part=169&division=div1.

34 *Norfolk Intelligencer*, 6 Sep. 1775; *Virginia Gazette* (Pinckney) 14 Sep. 1775. Pinckney added, *"those who are born to be H[ange]D will never be Drowned"* – thereby casting some doubt on whether the incident ever happened. It is, in any case, a good story, fully in keeping with rebel notions of Dunmore as a bumbling incompetent. See also, *Revolutionary Virginia*, 4: 4–5.

35 Earl of Dunmore to Earl of Dartmouth, 5 Oct. 1775, *Documents of the American Revolution, 1770–1783* (21 vols.; New York, NY, 1984) 9:137–138.

36 *Ibid.*, 9: 137. Allan was later tarred and feathered for behavior deemed inimical to the cause of liberty.

[37] Earl of Dunmore to Earl of Dartmouth, 22 Oct. 1775, *Documents of the American Revolution*, 9:161.

[38] Earl of Dunmore to Earl of Dartmouth, 6 Dec. 1775 – 18 Feb. 1776, *ibid.*, 12:58–60.

[39] Earl of Dunmore to Earl of Dartmouth, 22 Oct. 1775, *ibid.*, 9:162.

[40] *Virginia Gazette* (Purdie) 20 Oct. 1775.

[41] James Parker to Charles Steuart, 29 Oct. 1775, as quoted in *Revolutionary Virginia*, 4:7.

[42] Edmund Pendleton to William Woodford, Jr., 4 Jul. 1775 *Pendleton Papers*, 1:113–114.

[43] Captain Beesley Edgar Joel, on board the Otter, Norfolk, Virginia, to Mr. Joseph Wright, London (an intercepted letter), Oct. 1775, *Revolutionary Virginia* 4: 278; Samuel Edwards, Mate of the *Otter* to Unidentified Addressee (an intercepted letter), 8 Nov. 1775, *ibid.*, 4:344–346.

[44] John Pendleton, Jr., Clerk, Committee of Safety to William Woodford, 24 Oct. 1775, *ibid.*, 4: 269–270.

[45] Orders for Colonel William Woodford, *ibid.*, [24 Oct. 1775] 4:270–271.

[46] Anthony Warwick, Portsmouth, Virginia, to Messrs. Cuming, MacKenzie & Co., Glasgow (an intercepted letter), 10 Nov. 1775, *ibid.*, 4:370.

[47] Orders for Colonel William Woodford, [24 Oct. 1775] *ibid.*, 4: 270–271.

[48] For the orders cited in this paragraph, see, *seriatim*: Edmund Pendleton to Patrick Henry, Esqr. 24 Oct. 1775, *ibid.*, 4: 271; Edmund Pendleton to Patrick Henry, Esqr., "A Second Directive," 24 Oct. 1775, *ibid.*, 4: 272; Edmund Pendleton to Colonel Patrick Henry, 25 Oct. 1775, *ibid.*, 4:277.

[49] Quoted in *ibid.*, 4:8.

[50] Edmund Pendleton to Colonel Patrick Henry, 25 Oct. 1775, *ibid.*, 4:277.

[51] *Virginia Gazette* (Pinckney), 26 Oct. 1775. Thanks to Pendleton, we do know her next place of residence, however: the "Debtor's Room in the Great Gaol" in Williamsburg. Edmund Pendleton to Colo. Henry (subtitled, "a Second Directive"), 9 Nov. 1775, *Revolutionary Virginia*, 4:352.

[52] *Virginia Gazette* (Pinckney) 3 Nov. 1775.

[53] *Virginia Gazette* (Purdie), 3 Nov. 1775.

[54] Edmund Pendleton to Richard Henry Lee, 15 Oct. 1775, *Pendleton Papers*, 1:121.

[55] Earl of Dunmore to Earl of Dartmouth, 5 Oct. 1775, *Documents of the*

American Revolution, 9:138.

56 Edmund Pendleton to Thomas Jefferson, 16 Nov. 1775, *Pendleton Papers*, 1:130–131.

57 *Memoirs of Helen Calvert Maxwell Read*, Charles B. Cross, Jr., ed. (Chesapeake, Virginia, 1970), pp 52–53.

58 Neil Jamieson to Glassford, Gordon and Co., [17 Nov. 1775], (an intercepted letter, transmitted to Congress by Gen. Washington, with his letter dated 18 Dec. 1775.) *American Archives*, 4th Series, http://lincoln. lib. niu.edu/cgi-bin/amarch/getdoc.pl?/var/lib/philologic/databases/ amarch/.10261

59 Lord Dunmore to Lt. Gen. Sir William Howe, 30 Nov. 1775 (an intercepted letter), *Revolutionary Virginia*, 4:496.

60 Neil Jamieson to Glassford, Gordon and Co., [17 Nov. 1775], *American Archives*, 4th Series, http://lincoln.lib.niu.edu/cgi-bin/amarch/getdoc. pl?/var/lib/philologic/databases/amarch/.10261

61 John Brown, Norfolk, Virginia, to Mr. William Brown, Merch. London, 21 Nov. 1775 (an intercepted letter), *Revolutionary Virginia*, 4:446.

62 Earl of Dunmore to Earl of Dartmouth, 5 Oct. 1775, *Documents of the American Revolution*, 9:138.

63 "Most Infernal Misrepresentation That Ever Could Be Fallen Upon," (said to be in the hand of Landon Carter), Richmond County Committee, *Revolutionary Virginia*, 5:59–61.

64 John Ewing, Portsmouth, Virginia, to Mr. Thomas Ewing, 20 Nov. 1775 (an intercepted letter), *ibid.*, 4: 436;

65 Robert Shedden, Portsmouth, Virginia, to Mr. John Shedden, 20 Nov. 1775 (an intercepted letter), *ibid.*, 4:439.

66 *Memoirs of Helen Calvert Maxwell Read*, pp. 55–56.

67 Earl of Dunmore to Earl of Dartmouth, 6 Dec. 1775 to 18 Feb. 1776. *Documents of the American Revolution*, 12:57–68. The five letters under this cover are dated December 6 and December 13, 1775; January 4, February 13 and February 18, 1776.

68 *Virginia Gazette* (Pinckney) 20 Dec. 1775. It should be noted that the Grenadiers were trained to undertake assaults against fortified positions. That said, the insanity of a making a frontal assault up a narrow, unprotected causeway to a seven-foot high, well-defended redoubt speaks for itself.

69 Earl of Dunmore to Earl of Dartmouth, 6 Dec.1775 to 18 Feb. 1776,

Documents of the American Revolution, 12: 60.

70 *Memoirs of Helen Calvert Maxwell Read*, pp. 58–60.

71 *Ibid.*, p.60.

72 Quoted in *Revolutionary Virginia*, 5: 9–10; see also, "Extracts of Letters from the Committee of Safety in Virginia, dated Williamsburg, December 16," *ibid.*, 5:161.

73 Earl of Dunmore to Earl of Dartmouth, 6 Dec. 1775 to 18 Feb. 1776, *Documents of the American Revolution*, 12: 61.

74 Colonel William Woodford to the President of the Convention at Williamsburg, 11 Dec. 1775, *Revolutionary Virginia*, 5:109.

75 Gen. Washington to Col. William Woodford, 11 Nov. 1775, *American Archives*, Series 4, Vol. 3, p. 1428 http://lincoln.lib.niu.edu/cgi-bin/ amarch/ documentidx.pl?doc_id=S4-V3-P01-sp28-D0159&showfullrecord=on.

76 Quoted in *Revolutionary Virginia*, 5: 9.

77 Col. Patrick Henry to Col. William Woodford, 6 Dec. 1775, *ibid.*, 5:68.

78 Col. William Woodford to Col. Patrick Henry, 7 Dec. 1775, *ibid.*, 5:77-78.

79 *Ibid.* Woodford's obligation to periodically report to his commander in chief, is clearly stated in the Committee of Safety's order of 22 Dec. 1775. *Ibid.*, 5:221 and 225 n. 45.

80 The following account is based on Robert L. Scribner's Introductory Note to Volume V of *Revolutionary Virginia*, itself based on the letters of actual participants. See *Virginia Gazette* (Purdie) 15 Dec. 1775 and *Virginia Gazette* (Purdie) 20 Dec. 1775.

81 *Virginia Gazette* (Purdie), 15 Dec. 1775.

82 A street in Portsmouth, Billy Flora Way, was named after him. After the war, Flora operated a successful livery stable in his native town. He again volunteered for combat when British forces invaded Hampton Roads during the War of 1812. He retired in 1818 and died in Philadelphia.

83 *The Virginia Historical Register and Literary Companion*, William Maxwell, ed., (Virginia Historical Society, 1853), 6:5.

84 The sole rebel casualty at the Battle of Great Bridge was a slight wound to the hand of Capt. Thomas Nash of Portsmouth. But for Nash, whose recollections of the battle form the basis of the account published in *The Virginia Historical Register*, Billy Flora's heroics are unlikely to have

found their way into the history books.

85 Col. William Woodford to the President of the Convention at Williamsburg, 9 Dec. 1775, *Revolutionary Virginia* 5:90.

86 *Ibid.*, 5:21, n. 25.

87 Capt. Samuel Leslie to Lt. John Batut, *Virginia Gazette* (Pinckney) 13 Dec. 1775. Fordyce was described by Helen Maxwell as "not handsome, but very genteel, and I remember seeing him one day turn over Mr. M[axwell]'s music, of which he was very fond and humming some of the tunes."

88 Woodford's salute to the fallen grenadiers would later be returned in kind by the British, who interred him with full military honors when he died of sickness following the surrender of American forces at the Battle of Charlestown in 1780.

89 John Daly Burk, *The History of Virginia, from Its First Settlement to the Present Day* (3 vols.; Petersburg, Va., 1804–5), 3:446.

90 Richard Kidder Meade to Richard Bland, 18 Dec. 1775, *The Bland Papers, Being a Selection from the Manuscripts of Col. Theodorick Bland, Jr.*, Charles Campbell, ed. (2 vols.; Petersburg, Va., 1840), p. 39.

91 Quoted in *Virginia Gazette* (Pinckney), 13 Dec. 1775.

92 *Ibid.*

93 Burk, *The History of Virginia*, 4:87. (Burk having been killed in a duel in 1808, volume four of his work was ably carried on by Skelton Jones and Louis Hue Girardin, (Petersburg, Va. 1816).

94 Born on a plantation in Brunswick County, North Carolina, educated in England and, following his return in 1764, elected to the colonial assembly, Robert Howe owed his appointment as Colonel of the 2nd North Carolina Regiment to the prominence of his family. He was promoted to Brigadier General of the Continental Army on March 1, 1776, and on October 20, 1777, as Major General Howe, led a failed effort to capture St. Augustine in British Florida. He later saw action at Savannah and at Stony Point, and was transferred to the main Continental Army under Washington in January of 1781, where he put down a mutiny by executing two of the ringleaders. (Another mutiny in Philadelphia dissolved at his approach in June of 1783.) He returned to North Carolina a hero, was elected to the State Assembly and died, quite suddenly, on December 14, 1786. Howe had a reputation as a

womanizer. His comrades considered him pompous.

95 Col. Robert Howe to the President of the Convention at Williamsburg, 15 Dec. 1775, *Revolutionary Virginia*, 5:152–153; Colonel Robert Howe to the President of the Convention at Williamsburg, 17 Dec. 1775, *ibid.*, 5:169.

96 Capt. Matthew Squire to The Officers Commanding in Norfolk, [16 Dec. 1775], *ibid.*, 5:160.

97 Cols. Robert Howe and William Woodford to Capt. Matthew Squire, 16 Dec.1775, *ibid.*

98 Col. Robert Howe to the President of the Convention, 14 Dec. 1775, *ibid.*, 5:141;

99 Col. William Woodford to the President of the Convention, 14 Dec. 1775, *ibid.*, 5:142–143.

100 Cols. Robert Howe and William Woodford to the President of the Convention, 16 Dec. 1775, *ibid.*, 5:159.

101 Col. Robert Howe to the President of the Convention, 22 Dec. 1775, *ibid.*, 5:217–218.

102 Italics supplied. Cols. Robert Howe and William Woodford to the President of the Convention, 1 Jan. 1776, (with the notation "Norfolk, 10 o'clock at night"), *ibid.*, 5:308–309.

103 *Ibid.*

104 The wind being off the land, there was little likelihood that any fires started by Dunmore would spread to the city proper.

105 The burning of Norfolk is described in *Revolutionary Virginia*, 5:15–17. See also, the "Petition of Inhabitants of Norfolk and Princess Anne Counties, *ibid.*, 5:362–363.

106 *Journal of the House of Delegates of the Commonwealth of Virginia, Begun and Held at the Capitol . . . on Monday, the Seventh Day of December, One Thousand Eight Hundred and Thirty-five* (Richmond, 1835 [1836]) app., doc. 34, p. 16.

107 Col. Robert Howe to the President of the Convention, 2 Jan. 1776, *Revolutionary Virginia*, 5:319.

108 Col. William Woodford to the President of the Convention, 5 Jan. 1776, *ibid.*, 5:345–346.

109 Col. Robert Howe to the President of the Convention, 5 Jan. 1776, *ibid.*, 5:345–347.

[110] Burk, *The History of Virginia,* 4:110.

[111] Col. Robert Howe to the President of the Convention, 6 Jan. 1776, *Revolutionary Virginia,* 5:355–356.

[112] *Ibid.*

[113] Quoted in *ibid.,* 5:16.

[114] *Ibid.*

[115] *Ibid.*

[116] *Ibid.,* 5:16–17.

[117] *Ibid.,* 5:17.

[118] Earl of Dunmore to Earl of Dartmouth, 6 Dec. 1775 to 18 Feb. 1776, *Documents of the American Revolution,* 12:67.

[119] Quoted in *Revolutionary Virginia,* 5:17.

[120] *Ibid.,* 5:18.

[121] Edmund Pendleton to William Woodford, 16 Jan. 1776, *Pendleton Papers,* 1:148.

[122] *Virginia Gazette* (Purdie), 5 Jan. 1776 (Supp).

[123] Col. Patrick Henry to Col. William Woodford, 6 Dec. 1775, *Revolutionary Virginia,* 5:68.

[124] Col. William Woodford to Col. Patrick Henry, 7 Dec. 1775 *ibid.,* 5:77–78.

[125] Joseph Jones to William Woodford, 13 Dec. 1775, Quoted in *ibid.,* 5:225, fn. 45. According to William Wirt, Pendleton's (and Jones') principal objective in these negotiations was to keep Woodford (in Wirt's words) from "resigning in disgust." Pendleton was insistent that whatever solution Jones came up with it should make Col. Woodford "easy." "Believe me, Sir [he told Woodford, in the letter quoted on page 17 of this book] the unlucky step of calling [Henry] from our councils, where he was useful, into the field, in an important station, the duties of which he must, in the nature of things, be an entire stranger to, has given me many an anxious and uneasy moment. In consequence of this mistaken step, which cannot now be retracted or remedied, for he has done nothing worthy of degradation, and must keep his rank, and we must be deprived of the service of some able officers, whose honor and former ranks will not suffer them to act under him in this juncture."

[126] "An Instruction to Colonel Woodford," Dec., 1775, *ibid.,* 5:221.

[127] See letter from "Cato" in the *Virginia Gazette* (Dixon and Hunter), 30

Mar. 1776, laying out the entire story of Henry's career as Commander in Chief of Virginia's armed forces, from the debate over his appointment to his final resignation.

128 Edmund Pendleton to Col. William Woodford, 16 Mar. 1775, *Pendleton Papers*, 2:158.

129 *Virginia Gazette* (Purdie), 1 Mar. 1775.

130 *Ibid.*

131 *Ibid.*

132 *Ibid.*

133 *The Diary of Colonel Landon Carter*, Jack P. Greene, ed., (2 vols.; Virginia Historical Society, 1965, 1987) 2: 999.

134 Extract of a Letter from Colonel William Woodford to the Honourable the President of the Convention, 15 Dec. 1775, *Revolutionary Virginia*, 5:153.

135 Quoted in *ibid.*, 5:410–411, n. 5.

136 Earl of Dunmore to Lord George Germain, 26 Jun. 1776, *American Archives* Series 5, Volume 2, Page 0162, http://lincoln.lib.niu.edu/ cgi-bin/amarch/getdoc.pl?/var/lib/philologic/databases/amarch/.22384.

137 Earl of Dunmore to Lord George Germain, 30 Mar. 1776, *Documents of the American Revolution*, 12:101.

138 *Virginia Gazette* (Purdie), 19 Jul. 1776; see also, Peter Jennings Wrike, *The Governor's Island, Gywnn's Island, Virginia, During the Revolution*, (The Gwynn's Island Museum, Gwynn's Island, Va., 1995), pp. 78–88.

139 The description of Dunmore's thigh is derived from a friendly 1771 account describing him as "short, stocky and well built."

140 Lord Dunmore to Lord George Germain, 31 Jul. 1776, *American Archives* Series 5, Volume 2, Page 0164, http://lincoln.lib.niu.edu/cgi-bin/ amarch/getdoc.pl?/var/lib/philologic/databases/amarch/.22386.

141 Lord Dunmore to Lord George Germain, 6 Dec. 1775–[18] Feb. 1776, *Documents of the American Revolution*, 12:67–68.

142 Earl of Dunmore to Earl of Dartmouth, 6 Dec. 1775–[18] Feb. 1776, *ibid.*

143 *Ibid.*

144 *Virginia Gazette* (Purdie), 9 Aug. 1776.

145 George Morgan, *The True Patrick Henry*, (1907; Reprint, Am. Found. Pub., Bridgewater, Va., 2000), p. 271.

146 *Ibid.*, pp. 273–274. According to Morgan, Gov. Henry attended the first meeting of the new House of Delegates on Oct. 7, went home to Scotchtown shortly before Oct. 30, and did not return to Williamsburg until Nov. 19.

147 William Wirt, *Sketches of the Life and Character of Patrick Henry*, (1817; Kessinger Reprint, no date), p. 153.

148 *Ibid.*, p. 154.

149 *Ibid.*, p. 150–151.

150 Patrick Henry to Robert Pleasants, 18 Jan. 1773, Morgan, *The True Patrick Henry*, pp. 247–248.

151 Earl of Dunmore to Earl of Dartmouth, 6 Dec. 1775 – [18] Feb. 1776, *Documents of the American Revolution*, pp. 56–68, 62.

152 "Order for a Strict Inquiry," 31 Jan. 1776, *Revolutionary Virginia*, 6:40, 41, n. 4.

153 John E. Selby, *Dunmore*, (Virg. Ind. Bicent. Comm.; Williamsburg, Va., 1977), pp. 63–64, 68.

Acknowledgements

Dr. Samuel Johnson once said, "It is wonderful how a man will sometimes turn over half a library to make just one book." After ten years of nearly constant work on this series, I find that I have not only turned over half a library, but a good part of my life. New friends have become old ones. Some very good friends who read the essays in this series in their very earliest versions are now gone. Meanwhile, the library – I am speaking of the ever-expanding library of the internet – has only gotten larger.

It is impossible to name everyone who helped make this series, but some I must mention. There would be no series without the love, encouragement and help of my wife, Joan Morrow. But for the welcoming attitude, expert assistance and criticism of two truly fine historians of the period, Rhys Isaac and James Horn, I would still be trying to distinguish the forest from the trees. The encouragement I received from my two chief non professional readers, Joan and Terry Thomas, turned a mere collection of dates, people and events into a study of the character of Williamsburg. Other people who read one or more of the essays and made helpful comments include my 90-year-old aunt Rosemary Bauder, Paul and Joan Wernick, Richard Schumann, Bill Barker, Michael Fincham, Ken and Judith Simmons, Fred Fey, Cary Carson, Jon Kite, Al Louer, Bob Hill and Colleen Isaac. I also wish in particular to thank Jon Kite for obtaining the French army dossier of John Skey Eustace and for translating one of Jack Eustace's overwrought pamphlets from the French. Richard Schumann, James Horn and Roger Hudson kindly consented to do prefaces for one of the booklets in this series. Al Louer and Paul Freiling of Colonial Williamsburg arranged for me to see Williamsburg from the roof of the Governor's Palace, a view that put time itself in perspective .

Those who are subscribers to the British quarterly, *Slightly Foxed*, described on its website as "The Real Reader's Quarterly," will recognize some similarities between the booklets in this series and that magazine. The resemblance is no accident. When I saw *Slightly Foxed* for the first time, I immediately realized that it was the perfect model, in size, material and design for what I was looking for. With that in mind, I contacted Andrew Evans at 875 Design, the English book design firm responsible for its appearance, and asked him if would be willing to take on this project. He said, "yes," and it was not long before he and I had assembled a team of people who not only seemed to know what I wanted but were able to give me something I never expected to find: new ideas on the subject matter. I especially want to thank Gail Pirkis, the publisher of *Slightly Foxed*, for recommending Roger Hudson as editor for this series. Roger is not only a highly accomplished writer in his own right, he is truly a writer's editor.

Sadly, the genial spirit who presided over the series, read and commented on virtually every booklet and guided me through its development, died while the series was still in production. I am speaking of Rhys Isaac, the Pulitzer Prize-winning author of what is still the best book ever written on late colonial Virginia, *The Transformation of Virginia*. Rhys' presence at our dinner table will be deeply missed. But he will also be missed from the profession of history, where his exuberant writing style and elegiac approach to the past daily gave the lie to the sour souls who think history is about settling scores.

As I began these Acknowledgments with a quotation from

Samuel Johnson I would like to end with one *about* Johnson. It was spoken by someone who did not know him well, but knew of him very well, William Gerard Hamilton. For me, it is Rhys Isaac's epitaph: " He has made a chasm, which not only nothing can fill up, but which nothing has a tendency to fill up. – Johnson is dead. – Let us go to the next best; – There is no nobody; – no man can be said to put you in mind of Johnson."

About the Author

GEORGE MORROW brings a lifetime of experience to bear on the characters of the people featured in this series. He has been a university instructor, lawyer, general counsel for a *Fortune* 100 company, the CEO of two major health care organizations and a management consultant. He received his academic training in textual analysis and literary theory from Rutgers and Brown Universities. He lives in Williamsburg with his wife, Joan, and two in-your-face Siamese cats, Pete and Pris.

WILLIAMSBURG IN CHARACTER